I0837715

Seducing Men is a Piece of Cake!

The 7 Dating Secrets to Start Dating Your High Quality Romeo

Angeline Royer

Contents

Introduction

How many times have you seen a hot guy at your office or maybe a bar and everything in you wanted him to just come up and talk to you, but he didn't even notice you? Have you ever looked at a couple and thought, how did they get that right? Dating can feel like such a tricky game, there are so many rules, so many unforeseen circumstances and so many cheaters and users out there. It seems daunting just thinking about it. However, the fact still remains you want to have a relationship, you want to be one half of the cute couple taking a stroll in the park. That is a perfectly acceptable desire, we just have to get you there.

This book will be your guide. You will not only learn how to get guys to talk to you, but you will also learn how to gain the confidence you need to go up to a guy you think is cute. Once you are done reading this book you will be fully equipped to handle any dating situation, from getting the date all the way to having a healthy and successful relationship. All this information will be given to you in less than 150 pages, now that is pretty remarkable. You will be able to stop wondering what if and start living in the moment and building memories and relationships that will be fulfilling and fun.

My name is Angeline and I have spent a large portion of my life trying to get to the bottom of the problems that surround the male and female relationship. I have studied, experienced, cried, been frustrated and felt rejected after trying my absolute best to get the guy and make a relationship work. But I have also developed relationships, experienced great triumphs and found love. I have seen so many women struggling with love and relationships that I decided to become a dating and life coach to help you ladies out. Because there are so many women facing similar struggles all over the world, I decided to write this book to reach as many as possible. Every woman has so much hidden power that is just locked away waiting for her to open the door and let it out so she can experience what a full and joyous life really is.

Once you have gone through this book and mastered the concepts outlined in it, you will become the strong, confident woman you have always wanted to be. No guy will be able to take advantage of you and you will not fall for the users and players of the world. Your friends will look up to you and want to be the type of woman you have become, and men will be eager and excited to date you. You will be a woman who knows her value and who is empowered in the way she has always wanted to be.

There are countless success stories from people who follow my advice, many of whom I still hear from today. Women who were once shy, timid and never got the chance to be with the man they desired are now strong and confident, capable of getting the men of their dreams and creating beautiful relationships. Their lives have been forever changed and I want the same for every woman who picks up this book.

With the information that is now available you have the power to change your life from sadness to happiness, from being passive to being able to get what you want, from settling for the wrong guys to welcoming men into your life that treat you the way you should be treated. Your heart will change, your emotional life will change, and your life will improve.

There is a saying that goes, the older you are the harder it is to change bad habits. Don't wait any longer when you have the answers right in front of you. Decide that today will be the day your life will change and then go for it. You have all that you need, all you need to do is cultivate the will to do it. You don't need to be frustrated any longer, take the leap and you will not regret it.

The tips, tricks and guidance in this book will help you to break out of the cage that has been holding you back. You will be able to live a life that is free from the fear and frustration that has been plaguing you for so long. You no longer have to settle for mediocre but can strive for something better, for something amazing. This book contains all the advice you will ever need, no more running to your friends or Googling answers. It is all right here at your disposal, take advantage of it and jump into the pages that will result in a better, happier you.

1

What Are You Looking For?

Before you even start the dating process and look for Mr. Right you need to answer this important question: What are you looking for? It is all well and good to want to be in a relationship and have your dream man on your arm but many women skip this crucial step in the process and then only later on in the dating process realize maybe this guy is not for me.

To save yourself from the drama of getting with someone and then having to break it off soon after, make sure you know what you are looking for. I understand that many women don't really even know what they are looking for but that is ok. This chapter will guide you through all the important steps and questions you should be asking so that you can get a quality guy. The most important thing to remember is that you are looking for a high-quality guy who will treat you right, not just any guy that is willing to date you. Having standards should be the basis of your life and it will flow into everything you do.

What Do You Want in a Man?

One of the best things you can do for your dating life is to take a few moments, or even days if you need to, to really sit and think about what you want in a man. If you don't know what you want, you will never find the right fit and you will realize that you have the wrong guy much later on in the relationship. Ultimately it wastes your time and his time. What you need is to know the type of guy you want so that you can say no to anyone that does not fit your idea of a guy that is good for you.

You could start by making a list, writing things down is the easiest way to sort through your thoughts and decide what you want. Start by writing down everything you can think of. Everything that is important to you, everything you want in a man, don't worry about the details now. It may be physical characteristics, personality traits, habits, whatever you think will be part of that dream man.

For example, maybe you find yourself attracted to men who have curly hair, write that down. Perhaps you want someone who is financially stable, can make you laugh or pushes you to be a better person. Write that all down.

Now when you are done with this list it is probably going to be very long and we have to be honest, there really isn't such a thing as a 'perfect man'. The truth is that no man is molded specifically to a woman and there will always be something that you don't like about someone. Writing this list is not in vain or just to get your hopes up, but rather to see what you value in a person. Now that we have it all written down the next step would be to split this list into two categories: the non-negotiables and the nice-to-haves.

First let's chat about the non-negotiables, this category is the absolute must-haves in a man. Things that if he does not have then it will not work. This should be your shortest list as there shouldn't be too many non-negotiables otherwise you run the risk of being too rigid with what you want. I would say a safe number would be about three things but definitely not more than five. It is important to have these standards but also remember to not be unrealistic with them.

An example of a non-negotiable would be something like he wants to have kids or get married. These would be things that you won't budge on. Ask yourself where your values lie when thinking about this. Another example may be he is financially stable or is working towards that.

Things that should not be on this list is 'needs to be taller than me' or 'must enjoy running'. Although these things may be some things that you want, it really doesn't make that big of a difference in the grand scheme of your future or your relationship.

Next is the nice-to-haves, these are the things that you value and things that matter but at the end of the day you would be able to bend on them. Like I said before there is no such thing as a perfect person, so we need to be a bit flexible with certain things. Everything else on your list that did not make the non-negotiable list will fall into this category.

So things like physical characteristics can go here. As much as it would be nice to have a man with the physical attributes of Chris Hemsworth, there is only one of him and unfortunately, he is already taken so we can't be hoping for that one. But if this is something that you value then you may put in on the list. Look at the things that you enjoy doing since it would be nice to be with someone who enjoys the same things as you. There are many things you can put on this list, tailor it to you and be as honest and as realistic as possible.

Now that your list is all done, it's time to put it to work and use it. When going out on dates or meeting people you will already have your top non-negotiables so if any man does not meet that criteria you can eliminate him from the running. This does not mean they are a bad guy but rather he is not the guy for you and that is ok because there are many women who may really want that type of guy.

Don't use your nice-to-have list as the criteria but as you get to know the guy see what he has and what he doesn't. If he likes running and you like running that's a win for you. However, if he likes eating Indian food and you can't stomach spicy food then this should not be a deal breaker as it is something you can work around. You may even find that you will start having a new appreciation for things you did not like in the past.

Stop Falling for Bad Boys

Ahh the classic bad boy dilemma. I think every girl has been through it at least once. For some they have learnt their lesson and moved on and for others they find themselves in this perpetual cycle of falling for these bad boys. If you find yourself in the cycle, then it's time to break free. There has never been a fulfilling relationship that has come out of dating an emotionally unattached, player-type bad boy.

Now it is important to distinguish between a 'bad boy' and someone who is just bad for you. A bad boy is someone who is manipulative, strings you along and constantly makes you feel less than. You never really know where you stand with this type of guy. He can be sweet sometimes and then all of a sudden turn around and make you feel horrible about yourself. These types of guys usually aren't in it for a real relationship but rather for the fun of it. A guy that is bad for you is just a normal guy that may not share your same values, goals or outlook on things that are important; this does not make him a bad person but rather a different person than would fit for you.

Now that we have an idea of what a bad boy is, let's take some steps to getting out of these unhealthy relationships and as a result keep ourselves open to having long lasting, fulfilling relationships.

It's time to stop making excuses for him. Many women make excuses for the guys they are dating and if you ever find yourself justifying why you are with someone—either to the people close to you or to yourself—then this is a good indication that he is not good for you. Common excuses are, 'He's not like this when we are alone' or 'He is just angry; he isn't usually like this' or the classic 'He has so much potential'. At the end of the day if the people around you are questioning his character and motives, then maybe you should too. There is a high chance that they are seeing something you are not.

There are no valid excuses and you know that if you are completely honest with yourself. If you find yourself spending more time making excuses for his actions and behaviors than actually being proud to be with him and boasting about him, then it is time to move on to someone whose character speaks for him.

No matter what you do, you can't change him. Women have been trying to change men since the beginning of time and I think it is safe to say that it just does not work. No one should change a person; people should be in charge of themselves and that includes the men that you are trying to change. If we try to change someone then it is only a matter of time before they revert back to their old ways and then all our efforts have been wasted.

Bad boys are usually self-absorbed, and they only care about what is in it for them. There is no woman that can take a guy out of that mindset, so stop trying. The longer you keep trying to fix him, the more attached you will become to the idea that he can be adjusted because you have been invested for so long.

Dig deep and ask yourself, "why am I attracted to him?". There are quite a few reasons as to why you would be attracted to a bad boy. This does take some introspection because you cannot address the problem if you have no idea what it is. Take some time to really think about what you find so appealing about a bad boy and why you keep getting sucked into their false promises.

Perhaps you have an absent or emotionally unavailable parent(s), and this causes you to seek out the same in the men that you date. Sometimes even though it hurts us we still seek out the things that we know, rather than what is good for us. If this is the case for you, then you need to heal from this hurt, forgive your parent(s) who have hurt you or were just not there for you. This does not necessarily mean you have to go and find your absent father and hash out all the things he did to hurt you but rather actually dealing with your emotions for yourself. If it is possible to speak to your parents, then it would be a good option but if not then remember forgiveness and healing happens inside you and does not need another person to be present.

Another reason is that you may be in love with the fantasy of the bad boy. Bad boys are associated with being strong and being able to protect you and maybe you like that idea so much that you are unknowingly giving up important things so that you can have that fantasy. Maybe you want what you can't have; these types of men are emotionally detached and only care for themselves. They may lead you on but that's pretty much the extent of the relationship, there is nothing deeper there. The harder it is to get something, the more we want it. So, the woman will push and try harder to make something out of this relationship and the guy will distance himself and pull away even more. This results in the woman feeling like she has to chase even harder and the cycle continues until she is left hurt and broken at the end of it. This fantasy is exactly that, a fantasy, it has no place in real life and it is unsustainable.

There may be other reasons that are causing you to be attracted to him and you should write them down and see why you are so into this guy. If you write down things like 'he is so sexy' or 'our physical chemistry is through the roof' then you need to take some time to reevaluate this relationship. It's not that these things are bad, but they definitely are not the most important things and these things will not last in the long run and neither will the relationship.

As a woman, you need to realize that you are worth more than what you are getting. At the root of every bad, unhealthy, broken relationship lies two people. It's not the relationship that causes the problem but rather the people in it. Now, as already discussed, it is not your job or responsibility to change someone else, in fact it is nearly impossible, but it is your job to take ownership of yourself. If you believe that you are useless and not worthy of someone loving you, then the guys that you will be chasing are ones that will treat you according to your beliefs about yourself. What you put out is what you will receive and that is true in every context.

A woman who truly knows her worth and values herself will not let anyone tell her otherwise and she will stand strong in that conviction about herself. She will not settle or allow someone to belittle her, and if someone is treating her less than what she believes she deserves, then she would not be afraid to break it off with that person. That is the type of woman every woman should strive to be.

Understand that when you choose someone to be with, it is a direct reflection on the standards you believe you deserve. Believe that you are a person of worth and that means that you need to be with someone that treats you as such.

Don't Lower Your Standards

So many women are actually scared to have standards as they associate them with closing themselves off and they are scared that they will miss meeting their soulmate if they have them. Standards aren't meant to keep people out, but rather to allow the right people in. If you have rules, you aren't saying nobody speaks to me unless you meet the following criteria. Instead it allows you to eliminate the people that will not be beneficial to you and who could potentially cause you harm in the future.

Never be scared to set standards because they will protect you from wasting your time and getting hurt. There are a few common mindsets and ideas around standards that stop women from setting them and then sticking to them. We are going to discuss them below.

It's time to settle this: you aren't high maintenance if you have standards! We hear guys complaining all the time about top maintenance women. They say that women want and expect too much from them and many women are scared to be pegged as one of these high maintenance women. This is understandable as some women do take it too far and set ridiculous and unreachable standards, but the majority of us are able to set standards that are good for us and something that we should be expecting in a partner.

Wanting a partner who respects and cares for you is not too much of a high standard, it is exactly what we should wish to. Of course, the first step in this process is setting realistic and non-superficial standards and if you have these then your standards are not too high. A relationship should be uplifting and beneficial for both people in it, and if someone is not the type of guy that can give that to you, then you shouldn't be afraid to move on. In fact, the only men that will complain that you are high maintenance will be those that do not meet your standards and to be honest, you don't want them anyway. So, did you really lose anything? No, you didn't. In fact, you gained the freedom to be open to saying yes to someone who was better suited to you.

Recognize that you have time and you don't need to be rushed. Don't make decisions because you feel like your time is running out. Of course, it would be nice to have someone to share and build a life with, but is it really worth it to rush the process and then end up disappointed with the life you have at the end? It shouldn't be making any decision because you feel pressured or rushed, as that hardly ever turns out well.

Avoid any future pain by making clear decisions without the pressure of the clock staring you down. It would be so much better to get married to the man of your dreams at 40 than to have just rushed into something in your 20s because you were feeling lonely. Remember the feeling of loneliness is just that, a feeling, and it will pass so don't use it as your compass.

Remember that if you settle, you might actually miss your someone amazing. As soon as you decide to get into a relationship with someone, you close the door to all others that could have been. Now, this is how it should be and when we get into a relationship with someone who loves us and is ideal for us it is a good thing, but when we settle for just anybody, what happens is that we have now closed the door on other people that may have been perfect for us. The lesson being keep the door open until the right person walks through.

Don't close the door too early, future you is trusting that you make the right choices for her happiness. The worst thing would be to look back on your life and see that there was someone amazing for you, but you traded that in for something you could have in the moment. A moment is fleeting, so don't base your life on it. Having someone who is just there to fill space should not be good enough for you. In fact, it shouldn't be good enough for the other person either. When you settle, you may also be robbing that other person of the opportunity of finding someone who he truly would be a great fit for.

There are two lives in every relationship, and it is important to make sure that the decision to be together is suitable for both of you. Settling is not good for either of you. Hold out, be patient. There are great guys out there and they will cross your path, but you just have to make sure you are not distracted by a sub-par man, otherwise you will risk missing them.

One of the worst things in life are regrets, so don't leave yourself open to them. The thing about regrets is that you don't feel them when you are making a choice but rather many months or years later when you have an opportunity to look back. If you settle, you will regret it. In fact, it will cause more harm to you than the good you think you will get from being in a relationship.

It is much better to be single than have a life filled with regret. Imagine being married to someone and feeling more alone than ever. That is much worse than being single, so don't allow yourself into that situation. Regret breeds resentment. Resentment for yourself and resentment for the other person. It could actually lead to an unhealthy relationship down the line. I don't think anyone wants that for themselves.

At the end of the day, being single is great. So many people believe that being single is a type of punishment that they would not wish on their worst enemy. Of course, I'm being a bit dramatic but that is how some women act. If you truly feel that way about being single, then you have some sort of problem with yourself; there is something that you don't necessarily like about yourself or are insecure about and you are trying to cover that up with a relationship.

Being single is the opportunity of unlimited time to spend with and work on yourself. Now if you are completely secure in yourself and you actually like yourself, then there shouldn't be a problem. It is important to find fulfillment in being by yourself before you can even think about getting into a relationship. Being alone and being lonely are two completely different concepts, being in a relationship does not get rid of the feeling of being alone. In fact, it is much worse to feel lonely in a relationship, when you have someone that you are meant to share your life with, but there is so much emotional and mental distance between you that you start to feel lonely. That is why it is crucial to make sure you are secure with yourself first.

Being single is such a great time if you don't spend it wishing you were with someone but instead using it as a time to work on your relationship with yourself. The most important person you can invest your time into is yourself, and you should do that as often as you can. Find out who you are, what you like and do the things that you enjoy and that fulfill you. Life gets busy and we can often put ourselves on the backburner but rather take this time to invest and grow and see how much more confident you become. Become a person you like to be around.

2

Confidence - The Right Frame of Mind

When it comes to attracting the opposite sex and just being a more attractive person in general, the most important thing you can have is confidence. Confidence shows that you are worth something and if you believe that you are worth something, then others will believe it too. Whatever you think on the inside will be carried out on the outside and you will exude confidence and people will find you more attractive, not only

in a romantic way but overall.

In order to show off confidence, you have to feel confident. Sure, there are a few things you can do on

the outside that can help you with this, like dressing up, doing your hair or wearing make-up, but these things are all peripheral. They do not get to the root of the problem which is all on the inside. It starts with what you believe about yourself and what you feel about yourself. Once we are able to change these for the better, we will see a complete shift in our lives.

Pillars of Inner Worth

There are four pillars that hold up the structure to our inner worth. Inner worth is what we believe about ourselves, do we believe that we are valuable? If the answer is yes, then we have a high inner worth and therefore have a high level of confidence. If the answer is no, then we do not think highly of ourselves and it will show in the way we carry ourselves.

We need to strengthen these four pillars in order to grow in confidence. Every woman is valuable and unique in her own way, some have just forgotten. Many life experiences and challenges may change the way you see yourself, and as a result your trust in yourself takes a knock. It is possible to build confidence again after you have lost it. Even if you are someone who has just never been confident, it is still possible to learn that you are worthy and build up your confidence from there.

Let's take a look at the four pillars of inner worth that will help us look at ourselves and see someone who is valuable. All of these pillars start with self, that means they cannot be based on outside factors, but on you and yourself and you are the only one that can change them.

Self-esteem is the first pillar. It is what you believe about yourself; it is built upon respect and value for oneself. However many times our self-esteem can waver based on a situation or something someone said or did, should never be the case. If you feel this happening, then remember that you are the only one who has the power to take control of yourself and what you think of yourself. What other people say and do cannot harm you unless you allow it to, you have the power to block it out or turn it into something positive.

Your self-esteem will directly impact the immediate world, so the people and places that you are constantly around. If you have low self-esteem the impact you have on the people and things around you will either be non-existent or even harmful. Someone who has no impact, or a negative impact will never be able to reach their full potential and others will not want to be around them. That is the harsh truth, even though self-esteem starts off with self it does not end there.

Low self-esteem may even lead to self-sabotage and eventually self-destruction. It is essential to notice these behaviors if they are showing up in your life, so that you can stop it and change directions. Have you ever felt like you don't want to try because you know you will fail? Or you give up right at the beginning of trying something new? Have you been speaking negatively about yourself or to yourself? If you have answered yes to any of these questions, then you most likely have low self-esteem. The only person that can change that is you, and how you do that is by getting back in the ring. You believe that you can't do something because you give up too soon. Instead push through and give it your best, start trying again and you will see the rewards of this on the inside as well as the outside.

People who has high self-esteem will show up for themselves. When there is a project that needs to get done, they get it done because they know they can do it and that they are relying on them and other people are relying on them. They find the motivation to do things because they know their input is valuable and they are required. They are needed not only by others but by themselves. Someone with high self-esteem does not need validation from others because they have already received it from within. The thing is however, that they will receive praise and positive feedback from others because they are able to go the extra mile because they believe in themselves. This is the type of person everyone should strive to be, and that every person can be. Every person has intrinsic value which means that without even doing anything you are already valuable from the day you are born. Once you start believing that, then your self-esteem will increase and so will your confidence.

The second important pillar of inner worth is self-worth. When we look at the term *worth* it means the amount of value we place on something. Now if we have a low self-worth then it means we have placed a low importance on ourselves and if we have a high self-worth then we have placed a high importance on ourselves. If something is of high value then that means we can trade it for something of high value, so when we believe that we have worth then we will not settle for less than what we deserve because who would trade a diamond for a dog bone?

Knowing what our worth is means that our actions will be raised to the level of our worth. It allows us to say no to things that are not good for us or not beneficial to us and say yes to things that will be good for us. In relationships that means we will choose to spend time with people who offer something valuable to us because we know we can give them something useful in return. If we believe that we are of no value then we will settle for being in relationships that have no value and this can be detrimental to our self-esteem, do you see how they are all connected?

Once you have a high self-worth you won't allow things to just happen to you, instead you will have the confidence to take what you deserve. You will be able to stand up to someone who is not treating you right or be able to ask for that promotion or raise. You won't cower back and just accept things the way they are. The thing about self-worth is that the more you work on it the more your value grows. That means as you gain more self-worth you will be able to ask for things and expect things that are of a higher value. You never have to settle at the same level but rather you can keep growing and improving and increasing your value.

As soon as your self-worth drops, you start looking at yourself as useless and unworthy of things that should be yours. The direct result of that is that you let yourself go and stop taking care of yourself. If you ever find yourself in a space where you no longer want to take care of yourself and dress up and show up, then it is very likely that you have low self-worth. Make a decision to take care of yourself because things that are valuable deserve to be taken care of. You don't have to be where you want to be in life in order to think of yourself as worthwhile, but recognize that you have the power to get there. Know that not only are you valuable now but you are working towards your future value which is exponentially more than where you are now. Treat yourself now with all the worth that the future has, and you will see that you will start living up to that expectation.

Let's talk about our third pillar, which is self-trust. According to the Oxford Dictionary the definition of trust is the belief in the reliability, truth or ability of something or someone. When you trust someone, you believe that they really know you and want the best for you and that is the same for trusting yourself. Do you think that you have your best interests at heart, or are you scared and doubtful when you are faced with a tough situation or decision? This an important question to ask when determining whether you have self-trust or not.

At its core, a lack of self-trust will show up in your life as indecision. If you find that you take really long to decide simple things like where to eat, if you want to go to an event or not, or even what to wear, then this is a sign of a lack of self-trust. If you did really trust yourself then as soon as you are faced with a choice you would make it and believe that it was the best one for you. Think about when you trust another person, if they say something, it does not take long for you to decide to believe them or not or to just go along with their choices, because in your heart you know that they would never make a choice that would hurt you or be harmful for you. Chances are you don't even think about it but rather it's an automatic reaction to trust them. This is how it should be for us individually; we should trust and believe in ourselves almost instantly.

The indecision that comes with a lack of self-trust will hold you back from reaching your full potential since you will spend all your time thinking about things instead of doing them. If it's hard to make decisions on small things, when big decisions need to be made you will be paralyzed and that is not good.

At the core of every human is intuition and this is a gut feeling that you should be able to trust because it is your first reaction to whatever is happening around you. When you believe yourself, you will be able to act on this gut feeling almost immediately. In order to cultivate self-trust, try to listen to that gut feeling. When you are faced with a decision ask yourself, 'how do I feel about this?' and once you have your answer make a decision. Don't overthink it but rather count to five and choose. Start doing this with smaller, more inconsequential things so that you can build up trust and eventually you will be able to make big decisions without having to constantly wrestle and justify yourself.

The final pillar is self-love. Love is putting someone first, taking care of them and being concerned for their wellbeing. This type of love needs to be cultivated for ourselves, but sadly many people do not have it. When someone loves themselves, they treat themselves with respect and don't let others belittle them, they know they are worthy to be loved, so they refuse to be treated otherwise.

Many women lack self-love, sometimes it's due to someone like a parent and leader they looked up to putting them down for a personality trait or physical attribute. This directly affects someone's confidence. When it is a deep-rooted issue, it needs to be solved at the core, you need to find out why you don't love yourself and deal with that.

The most powerful thing you can do is accept yourself. Accept every part of your body, from your fingers to your toes, accept your personality, your voice, your height. Accept yourself for who you are, that is the first step to loving yourself. If you find yourself speaking or thinking negative things about yourself, stop and replace that with something positive. Start training yourself to think about the good and accept the things that you may not like because even though they may not be your favorite parts about you they still make you *you* and they need to be celebrated.

Once you learn to love yourself then it makes it easier for others to love you because you aren't relying on someone else to make you feel loved and accepted; you already have that for yourself. You will be able to grow in confidence and others will see that. But remember the goal is not to get others to love you but rather that you love yourself regardless of what others think or do, it does not affect the way you see yourself or your confidence.

Overcome Social Anxiety and Shyness

Anxiety and shyness are something that many people struggle with. They are traits that many people carry around with them and are never able to fully work through or get over. Many people believe that these are just part of their personality and therefore they can't change them. This is a false belief because if you are willing to put in a little work you will definitely be able to overcome anxiety and shyness. When people are friendly, easily approachable, and easy to talk to it opens up a world of opportunities for them. Life is built around other people and relationships, so it is essential to move past shyness in order to really reach your full potential.

Let's dive into what shyness and social anxiety are. At their core anxiety and shyness are just fear of people. Fear that they will judge you. Fear that they will not like you. Fear that they won't accept you. Fear that they will ask you something you don't know the answer to. Whatever this dread is to you, at the root you are scared of what people think. This fear can hold you back from fulfilling relationships and even reaching your goals.

Many people mistake shyness for being an introvert. This is not true since not everyone who is introverted is actually shy. Someone who is introverted just needs time to be by themselves to recharge but once they have a full tank of energy then they are ready to go and can handle social situations as well as any extrovert can. If you are an introvert, you may think you are shy because you are quieter and you enjoy your own company, but that does not equate to anxiety or shyness. Introverts are more likely to be shy because they have been labeled as such and then they start to believe it. Don't allow that to happen to you. If you are an introvert recognize that it is ok to be by yourself but then allow yourself to be friendly and push yourself out of your comfort zone when you are in social situations.

Being shy or having anxiety is not a personality trait, it is something that can be changed. It is important to not accept anxiety or being shy as something that you cannot change. It is a mindset that is often caused by overthinking things, worrying what people will think if you say this or do that, being concerned that you will make a fool of yourself or that you are not smart, pretty or cool enough for people to like you. This can all be changed once you start doing a few things to change the way you feel and think.

We need to know how to overcome shyness and anxiety before we can do anything about them. Overcoming social anxiety and shyness is so important because people are everywhere, so you need to be able to deal with them with confidence. The truth is that people really aren't thinking about you; they are too busy thinking about themselves. Most people are insecure about something so if anything, they are consumed with thoughts of trying to look cool themselves rather than worrying about you and what you are doing. So, don't be scared to do something just because of people, especially if you are in a situation where you may not ever see those people again.

If you find yourself getting anxious or shy in social situations, then a you may start showing a few behavioral symptoms:

- Distancing yourself from people

- Keeping quiet and not speaking up

- Not making eye contact with others

- Leaving the social gathering early

Physical symptoms may be:

- Shaking or trembling hands

- Sweating

- Increased heart rate

- Mind going fuzzy and not being able to think straight

- Deep urge to leave or escape the situation

When you find yourself showing any of these signs, it is important to not let them control you. You are still in control; this is your life and this feeling does not own you. It might be a good idea to find a quiet spot, maybe an empty room or the bathroom where no one will bother or interrupt you for a few minutes. Close your eyes and think of something calming, perhaps a stream of running water, nature or whatever calms you. Then take a deep breath and slow your heart rate. Breathe through your nose, in for three seconds and out for three seconds. Keep repeating until you feel you have calmed down. The next step is the most important, go back to the social situation and try again. This time incorporating your breathing exercises while you are there if you feel anxious again. Don't worry, people won't really notice you doing anything different because it is just breathing. When anxiety takes hold of you, try not to run away. Taking a break may be good but running away never is a good idea. If you try to escape every time you feel anxious then you give that feeling more power over you than it should have. You are in control and the power is yours.

A few practical things you can do to help you overcome anxiety or shyness and build your confidence in the long run are:

Wear mismatched clothing - You can do this by wearing two different socks, two different earrings or gloves, anything that you have in your cupboard. Go out to the mall or park for the day and see how many people notice or stare at you because of it. The chances are very few, if any. This exercise is done to show you that people really aren't noticing or focusing on you as much as you may think. They will be too wrapped up in their own worlds to notice that you are wearing something funny.

Ask for the time - Again at a mall or park, wherever there are a large number of people, go around and ask random people for the time. This is a non-threatening question; it has nothing to do with you or them. Yes, some people may just walk away and not want to give you the time, but this will help you to deal with rejection in a non-personal way and see that it really isn't that bad. The more you do it the more confident you will be. You should try and ask about 20 people and you will see your confidence building. It will get more comfortable every time and soon you won't even have to think about it. Confidence takes practice so you need to be willing to do a few things repeatedly.

Go for it - This next one is definitely more dramatic than the other two suggestions but no doubt, it is the most effective. It is called radical implosion, and it means doing the thing that scares you until it just doesn't anymore. Pick something that you really are scared of doing, maybe it is talking to men, or singing in front of people, or perhaps you fear people looking at you. Do those things. Go up to random men in a mall and just say hi. Join in on a karaoke night. Wear the most absurd outfit so that people are forced to stare at you as you walk down the street. Yes, this is scary and yes, you may even feel like throwing up afterwards but once you have done this nothing else will seem so frightening. So when you are faced with a social situation you will be able to tell yourself that you can do it because you were able to say hi to 100 random men and if you are honest with yourself nothing bad actually happened beside a few weird looks.

Another way to overcome anxiety is by using exposure therapy. Anxiety is something that ¼ of the population in America deal with or have dealt with at some point in their life (Kaplan & Tolin, 2011). That is a big chunk of the population. Because of this there have been many studies done on the matter and they have found that exposure therapy is one of the most effective ways to combat anxiety. Once you come into contact with the thing that scares you the most, you have no choice but to deal with it. The goal is to show you that you can handle a big fear then when you are faced with something else that is scary in your life it won't feel that bad and you will have the courage to overcome it. If you really struggle with anxiety, it could be worth your while to do some research on it and maybe speak to a medical professional who would be able to guide you on the topic.

3

What Do Men Like, and How to Make Him Want You

Everyone wants to be wanted. There is a desire in all women to be wanted by someone and to be cared for by someone. Thank goodness men actually do want us. Men and women are naturally drawn to one another, but there are a few things that attract men and then a few that repel them. If we want to be successful in dating, then it is important for us to know what men find attractive and what men don't care for.

What Men Want in a Woman

Every man is different which means that each man would want a different type of woman. Everybody has preferences but there are specific things that, for the most part, men find attractive and want in a partner. These are the things men look for when searching for a long-term partner, it can vary between men but in my experience, it has been fairly consistent.

This list does not highlight a specific 'type' of woman but rather something that all women can have, even if some have to work on it a bit harder. It will not only make you more attractive to a man that you are interested in, but people in general will find you more likable and easier to be around. Implement these things and you will have men begging to date you.

Men want a woman who is attractive; they are visual creatures and that is how they are stimulated. They see something that they are attracted to and they want it. Many women have been offended by this statement since they don't believe that it is right to judge by appearance, but the truth is that the measure of beauty that women measure themselves to is not the same as what men use. You really don't have to be a Victoria's Secret model to be found attractive. Holding yourself to unfair beauty standards will actually hold you back in the long run.

That being said there is something to be said about preferences, because if you were going to say that you find every man attractive then you would be lying. This is the same with men, some men are just attracted to certain things and maybe you don't have that specific characteristic and that is OK. Instead of focusing on that, focus on the fact that there are thousands of men that will find you attractive.

Attractiveness is not just about your physical features or your body, but about the way you take care of yourself. You need to be the most attractive version of yourself.

- Make an effort to get dressed and ready every day and wear nice clothes that are good quality; take pride in what you put on. Choose pieces that are flattering to your body type, skin tone etc. The options for clothing are truly endless, you are bound to find something that matches your taste and looks good on you as well.

- Take care of your body. Now nobody says that you have to have the body of an athlete but take pride in the way your body looks. Eat well and try to find an exercise that you enjoy. This is not a tip to lose weight but rather to be happy and comfortable in your body.

- Decide that you want to be someone who is attractive. You need to have a confidence about you that translates from the inside to the outside. How you feel on the inside will always directly show up on the outside.

A Man also wants a woman who shares the same interests as him. Every man is passionate about something whether it is a job, hobby or something else. When he does this specific thing, it makes him light up and enjoy his time and life all the more. Men want a woman who has a similar passion to him. Someone who he can share his passion with and then work towards the goals he sets with that person. Even if it is just a hobby, he wants to enjoy that hobby with the woman he is with and be able to talk about it and know that she is enjoying it as much as he is.

Perhaps there are things that he likes to do that you are not a big fan of, that's ok because you can still support him and be interested in the things that are important to him. Where the line needs to be drawn is when you have different goals and dreams. Goals and dreams are more important than hobbies because they pave the way for the future and a man wants someone who wants the same things as him. He is thinking about the future and wants to build a life with someone who is moving in the same direction as him.

Men love women who will listen to them. As a woman we all want men who will listen to us and care about what we have to say. This is a two-way street as men want this as well. They want someone who will be interested in their stories and want to hear what they have to say. When a guy opens up, it shows that he wants to bond with you, so if you aren't paying attention or shut him down, he will retract and might not want to share with you again.

I know sometimes it can be so hard to listen because us women love to talk but slowing down and allowing him the chance to speak and open up will do wonders for your relationship. You don't even necessarily have the answers for him, but just being a listening ear and a shoulder for him to lean on will make him feel like you really do care about what is going on in his world.

The next thing men want in a woman is ambition. Contrary to popular belief, men actually want a woman who has her own dreams and goals and is actively working towards them. It shows that she will be a great partner and that she is not lazy. At the end of the day when you get into a relationship it is a partnership and men want to have the most advantageous partner on their side. Someone who sees a bigger picture and is willing to work for it.

As much as it is important to have similar goals, it is also important to have your own goals and vision for your life and be willing to work for that. In a man's mind if you aren't willing to work for your own dreams, there is no way that you would help and be supportive of him.

Not only that, you need to have your own life apart from his. Men don't like women who are too clingy. Having your own goals and own life outside of his is so important as it shows that you actually value yourself and other relationships in your world.

Men love happy women and it is something they find really attractive. A woman who is happy is something that is instantly attractive, she creates a good vibe to be around and makes the atmosphere fun! Think about it: Would you rather be around someone who is a drain or someone who has a good energy around them? What you put out affects the people around you. I'm sure you have been around someone who is just constantly in a bad mood. These people drain the life from any social situation, and nobody wants to be around them.

Create a vibe around you that is happy and fun, people around you will appreciate it and it will make you more attractive. Some men tend not to think about things long term and think about them as they are now. If being around you makes him feel good now, then he will be instantly drawn to you. Smile, laugh, joke, everyone around you will be affected by your mood and demeanor.

Another thing men want is a woman that is sexy. Let's just be honest here, men love sex. It is on their mind quite often and they want to be with someone who makes them want to have sex with them. When you will allow that to happen is totally up to you but being sexy should always be a part of flirting and showing a man that you are interested.

Showing a cheeky smile or saying something a little naughty will guide his mind into thinking of you more than a friend and that is what you want. You want him to think of you as a romantic partner. Don't be ashamed to flirt a little, even if you are well into the relationship, this is something that you should always be doing.

Most men want a woman that is playful. Someone playful and fun is instantly attractive in a man's eyes. Life is already so serious and that is no fun. Having someone who can take him out of the seriousness of life and remind him of the fun side is something every man wants.

Crack a joke or break out into a silly dance. Don't be afraid to look silly, most guys are goofy at heart so they want someone who will be goofy with them. It shows them that you don't take life too seriously and are open to doing things regardless of what other people think. Making someone laugh is the quickest way to their heart.

Another thing men love is someone who cares for them. As tough as a man may pretend to be, they are all big babies that need a little TLC. Men want to be taken care of as much as women do, it shows them that you are there for them and support them. Taking the time to do something for the guy you like will go a long way, especially if you know he has had a tough day or week.

Be someone he can lean on, check on him a few times a week, help him out in any way that you can. Obviously don't overdo it but make sure that he knows that you care about him and his wellbeing.

Lastly, men find women who have their own lives really attractive. Women tend to get so caught up in relationships with a guy that they neglect their relationships with their friends and family. This can lead to her becoming clingy and to a guy nothing is worse than a clingy girl. Guys need their space. It makes them enjoy your company all the more when they get the chance to spend time with you. This time apart creates a sense of missing you and that will draw him to you all the more. If you are constantly with him every single day, day in and day out, there is no chance for him to realize that he misses you or want to be around you because you are always there. People have a tendency to take for granted things that are just always there.

Show him that you are valuable by having other relationships and your own life outside of him. Play hard to get but have something to do when you are doing this. He needs to get the sense that you are a busy woman but are still willing to give up some of your time for him.

How and What to Talk About

Many women get stuck on what they should talk to a guy about and how to go about that communication. No need to stress out about that, it really isn't that hard. Men are just people too and they want to be talked to as such. Don't get too in your own head when it comes to this, talking is natural. However, I have highlighted a few guidelines to help make the process a little smoother.

The first thing you should do is ask questions. Starting a conversation can be daunting since you want the person to find you interesting and engaging. The trick here is that it is not about you, it is about the guy. Everyone wants to talk about themselves, it's who they know best and a topic that they will be well versed in.

Before you are able to tell him about you, you should open the floor to get him talking about himself. Ask questions about him, what he likes and dislikes, favorite foods, cars, etc. You can find out about what he is passionate about and what he does for fun. The more you know about him, the easier it will be to start a conversation with him in the future, since you now have something to build from.

Always try to be funny and light-hearted. Make jokes and lay around, this is especially important in the first few interactions because you will not have earned enough of his trust for you to get to the deeper stuff. The best way to a man's heart is by making him laugh. Don't think too much about it rather just let it flow out naturally. I'm sure you have heard a few good jokes or stories; you can definitely keep those in the back of your mind but try not to make it forced. Men will notice if you are just reading from a mental script.

You can even poke fun at him. Men are not as sensitive as women, so don't feel shy to jokingly pick on something he does or is wearing. Just don't sound condescending, you can even give him a little push or shove to indicate that you are just joking.

You could also bring up the topic of music and movies. Everybody likes music and watching movies so if you are ever stuck for a topic of conversation this is a great option. Ask for recommendations and why he likes that genre of music or that specific movie. Tell him about things that you have watched and like to listen to and give him recommendations. You can use this information in later conversations by saying something like, "Thanks for recommending this movie, I really enjoyed it when..." and you can just continue the conversation from there. These types of conversations are non-threatening since they are not about him personally so if you are dealing with a guy who is a bit more reserved or closed off then this might be the way to go.

Another great thing to bring up to get the conversation flowing is current events. Men pay attention to the world around them, especially once they have passed the 25-year mark. They engage with current events and news; you will find many men standing around and chatting about the news and what is going on in the world around them. It is important for you to also stay up to date with what is going on in the world around you since it will allow you to have opinions on the subject.

Having this information on hand will really help you when speaking to groups of guys since you will be able to contribute something, and it really will make you look smarter. Guys love a girl who is smart and cares about what is happening in the world around her instead of just focusing on her small bubble.

Lastly, make whatever you are saying actionable. When speaking try not to just say things that will just get a *yes*/*no* answer or a *thank you*. Choose sentences that will cause him to engage with you rather than just give an answer and then move on. The goal is to start a conversation, not just get a few words out and hope for the best. Ask open-ended questions that would make it easy for him to continue talking.

You are allowed to make your statements slightly negative since it is easier to make it actionable if it is leaning more to the negative side. Do it in a cheeky way so that he will not get offended. Say something like, "You look really great today, there's just something off. I just can't put my finger on it." It's a compliment but he won't be able to just say thank you and move on, he now wants to know what is the thing that is off and he will engage in a conversation with you because he wants to find out what was off. Now you know that there is nothing off about him so you can choose how to play your hand from this point on. You can go for the I was just joking approach, you can keep him guessing or you can try and give him another compliment, whatever you choose, make sure that you will be able to carry on the conversation from that point.

Physical Contact

Men love to be physical and it takes the relationship from just friends to something more. If you are interested in a man then it is best to start off the physical contact as soon as possible, that way you have less of a chance of ending up in the 'friend zone'. Try introducing little things so that you are not being intrusive but are still making it known that you are attracted to him. Also remember it is all about confidence, don't be nervous; there is a very high chance that he will love it.

This first tip is not actually about physical touch, but it can definitely lead to it if done correctly. Many women struggle with holding eye contact with a guy since it may feel a little awkward, but when you do hold eye contact it signals to a guy that you are interested and confident. Don't underestimate the power of eye contact.

It does not have to be for a ridiculously long time (otherwise it could get borderline creepy), but four to five seconds should be sufficient. Give him a little smile and then look away, this is the best way to intrigue him.

Once you have started the conversation with him, it is still important to maintain eye contact. It will show that you are interested and engaged with what he has to say. Try and look away a few times within the conversation so that he has to work to get your attention back. There is nothing wrong with playing a little hard to get once you have started a conversation with him.

Try touching his arm or shoulder. When you touch a man on his arms and shoulders it indicates to him that you are interested in him. You are considering taking this further but not yet 100% sure of it. It is almost the gateway of physical touch; it is generally the safest place to touch someone and you will be able to gauge if he is interested by the way he responds to it.

Reach out and touch his arm and just let your arm linger there for a little before you remove it. This will make him notice that you are touching him in something more than just a friendly way. You can even give his arm a light squeeze if you feel comfortable doing so.

The next step up from touching his arm or shoulder is touching his hand. When you touch a man on his hands that indicates that you are definitely interested in him and you want to see where this goes. Naturally in conversations with someone you find attractive your hands will move closer and closer together, once your hands are close enough, just lightly brush your fingers on his and see his reaction. If he doesn't move his hand away, then this is a good sign.

If you are unsure of how to touch his hand, try comparing hand sizes. In a more casual and playful situation there are other ways to get him to touch your hand. One of these ways is the hand comparison trick. First compliment him on his hands and then ask to see whose is bigger, yours or his. Of course, it would be his, but this is just a way to open the door to more physical touch.

Something else you could try in a more casual setting is the interlocking high-five. This can be done in a casual conversation, when he mentions something good about himself or an achievement, go in for the high-five then immediately interlock your fingers while making eye contact with him. This is also a non-threatening way to introduce touch, especially early on in the relationship when you are just getting to know each other.

Something you can introduce after you have been talking for a while is holding hands. It usually works best when you two are walking somewhere because then your hands will be at your sides and close to one another. There are two ways to go about this, the first approach is a more reserved one where you just allow the back of your hands to touch as you are walking. This one leaves the ball in his court since he needs to make the move to pick up your hand and hold it; you are merely letting him know you want him to hold your hand.

The second way is more direct, just ask him! After walking for a while, you will gauge whether he likes you or not then just say something to the effect of, "You know, my hand isn't going to hold itself!" Sometimes guys need a bit of guidance when it comes to these things.

If you have a ring, bracelet or watch on, then make conversation around it so that he will want to see it. He should pick up your hand to have a closer look. Don't forget to try and catch his eye and have a bit of eye contact before he puts your hand down.

Try to sit next to him because if you are sitting next to him at a bar or on a bench somewhere it makes it easier to do everything else that has been mentioned. This way there is no barrier between you, and you can also sneak in a leg to leg touch. This type of touch is constant and will make sure he knows that you are there since he can constantly feel you.

Men love their arms that's why the classic bicep arm touch is a tried and true flirty move. Making an excuse to touch his bicep is one of the oldest tricks in the book, and that is for good reason. It works! Compliment his arms and ask if he works out, whatever will get him to flex his biceps, then just use this as the opportunity to give them a squeeze. Alternatively, you can talk about how much you've been working out and how big your muscles are, which will get him to touch your arms and you can easily segue into comparing biceps.

As you progress you should try to touch his head and neck. The head and neck area are a vulnerable place so if he lets you touch him there then it's almost guaranteed that he wants to kiss you. It means he trusts you and wants to go further with you. You could try and just move a stray hair next to his ear and then move down to his neck. Other than that, you will just have to go for it, there aren't many tricks on this type of touching since it is already sensual, the slower you move the more tension you will build.

If things are going well then you can move on to something more intimate, the thigh touch. A touch on the inner thigh definitely signals that you are thinking about having sex with him. This move can definitely lead to something more, so don't do it unless you are really interested in that something more. You will have to gauge what he is comfortable with, as it depends on the type of guy he is. In my experience I haven't met many guys who complained about this so you can even cheekily slide your hand up to stimulate him a little more.

This last one never fails. If you have already built up some sort of relationship with him, playfully overpower him. Men like to be teased and challenged so use this to your advantage. Say something like, "I bet I can beat you at an arm-wrestling competition," or "It won't take much for me to pin you to the floor." He will most likely ask you to prove it and that's when you try to jump him or grab his arm. He will probably win, but the goal here is to get a little bit physical and break the touch barrier a bit more. As soon as the touch barrier is broken you allow yourselves to enter into another sphere of the relationship. There will be more intimacy both emotionally and physically.

4

Society and Sex

We are living in a very different time than what humans have experienced before. There is a lot of sex in the media and many images, and music videos are over-sexualized. We can hardly watch anything without a hot sex scene in it or a half-naked girl coming across the screen. After the sexual revolution in the 70s people's views on sex have changed and we are living in a shift between what was and what is now.

Society has a big impact on how people view sex and decide how to use their sexual freedom. Both women and men are affected by it but in different ways. Even though society does play a huge part in how people look at sex and live out their sexuality, it is important to recognize that it is your body and every individual needs to make the decision on it by themselves on what is best for them.

Prejudices About Sex

Even though both men and women are affected with the way sex is portrayed in the modern world, it seems to have affected women more negatively than men. We see women being overly sexualized in the media and men having this almost entitlement to sex whenever they want it while women are be labeled negatively no matter what they choose to do. If they have many sexual partners, then they are a slut, but on the other hand if they choose to not have sex or limit their sexual partners, then they are labeled a prude. Now I am not saying that men don't struggle with similar things around sex and sexuality, but we can see that it is more prevalent among females.

So, the big question is, why is this? Why are women shamed no matter what they choose and why do men hold so much power when it comes to a woman's sexual choices? The answer is the generation that we are living in. I know, not the answer you would expect but there have been many studies done on this. We can see in the late 1700s to the 1800s that there were more stable marriages and women were happy, there wasn't much abuse or over sexualization. Fast forward to the 1970s and we see marriages crumbling and divorce rates escalating. Sex started becoming a common topic and was done with little to no commitment. Women were being abused more and men were exerting their sexual preferences while women just fell into that mold. What changed?

We see that in the 1800s a woman's preference in relationships showed up more, women want to be cared for and loved in a stable relationship. As we move on in the years, we see that the male preference for 'relationships' becomes more prevalent. This model is more free sex and less commitment. The reason for this is that previously there were many more males than females, and that meant women had the power because in order to get a woman to be with you, you had to be the better man. Women had more options so if they felt like they weren't going to get what they deserved from a relationship, they had many other options available. They could be picky, and men would follow the model that they set out. Presently there are more women than men, on an average college campus in America there are about 100 women to every 70 men. This means that the tables have turned, and men now have the power in terms of how they want to handle relationships. They have more options, so if a woman does not want to give him what he desires, he can go and find it in another woman.

Now this is not said to demonize men or to make women feel like victims to society. It is just stating what the studies have shown and how we have adapted through the years. Now, this is unfortunate especially if you are a more traditional woman, but it isn't the be all and end all. At the end, of the day you are in control of your own body and your expectations in a relationship. These facts are not meant to demoralize you but rather to explain why it seems so difficult for women in relationships and why views on sex have changed so drastically over a few hundred years.

Let's take a look at how this plays out in the present day. Women feel loved when they are taken care of and spent time with whereas men are driven by physical stimulation and sex. We can see this in the animal kingdom as well where the males of the species go out of their way to mate with as many females in order to pass on their genes to as many offspring as possible. The females of the species usually don't share that same sentiment.

Because of the way society is structured now, women have adapted to the way of life that is presented to us. People are adaptable so we will usually just adapt to the way the world moves at that time. As much as the current model may not be ideal for some people, it does give others the freedom to be and what they please. If you feel bogged down with labels put on them by other people when it comes to sex, then shake them off; the only person that should have any say in the matter is you and you are in control of your own body.

Choose what you want, do you want to be more free sexually? Would you rather have fewer sexual partners or even save sex until marriage? The choice is up to you, nobody else has control over you in that aspect and the opinions of others should never matter since they are not going to be involved in your sexual life. The reality is that more and more people are having sex with multiple partners and if you feel that is right for you, then go for it. But if you feel that is not what you want to do then don't feel pressured into it.

It's not about the numbers, so don't feel pressured to count how many sexual partners you have had. If somebody asks, you are under no obligation to tell them. This comparison game is what creates this feeling that we should be having more or less sex and that creates shame. Don't worry about what other people are doing, focus on yourself and if somebody does not want to be with you because you have had too many or too few sexual partners, then it is their loss and you should find someone who has a better criteria for the people he would like to be in a relationship with.

If you are sexually active, then please use protection. Use a condom. I know many people don't really like using a condom but the truth is it is better to use one and be assured that you will be safe from STDs than not use one and have to live with an STD for the rest of your life.

Be smart and be safe.

Don't allow society's stigmas and prejudice to influence you. Decide what you want and what you expect and stick to that. This way you will remove the guilt and shame so many women suffer with. Don't allow others to shame you, the truth is that the people that choose to judge and shame are people that are also going through their own hurt and possible shame. Be kind to the people around you, even if you don't agree with their choices. It doesn't mean you have to force them to think the way you do. We should all be a society that cares about others and minds our own business.

The Good Girl Complex

Many women find themselves stuck in a good girl complex, but they actually don't know it. Good girls are people pleasers and they try to keep everyone around them happy, they keep their opinions to themselves and don't offend anyone. This is definitely something that is found mostly in women and it can translate into your dating life. You will always want to please that person and make sure they are ok at the expense of yourself.

I know what you are thinking, 'this chapter is

supposed to be about sex'. The truth is that the way we see ourselves will be the way we represent ourselves sexually. It will affect how we handle our sexuality and how we treat others with differing views. It will also determine how men and other people treat us both sexually and in general. If you do find yourself stuck in the good girl mindset, then the next few pages will help you to recognize it and change it in your own life.

Good girls are made, not born. Females who have a good girl complex have been trained to be so by circumstances and people in their lives. Although men and women are not the same, we have many differences, but we all start off in the same place. Yes, circumstances are different, but it is interesting to see how boys and girls from the same family can turn out so differently.

Stats were pulled on MBA students and they showed that only 7% of women who completed their MBA tried to negotiate their salary with their employers whereas well over 50% of men attempted to negotiate their salaries (Newsonen, 2018). That is a big gap and what is the reason? Both the males and females had the same qualifications and experience. This is a good example of how the good girl complex can hold you back in life. Trying to be a good girl and not rock the boat will leave you not getting what you deserve.

We can see the differences in society as men and women get older but what really causes this good girl mentality and strong man mentality? Well it can be taken back to when we are growing up. When we are young, girls naturally mature faster than boys so there is this higher standard placed on us. Parents often tell their daughters to act like a lady, be mature, take care of your brothers and younger siblings, whereas young boys don't have the same pressure on them; when they are rowdy or make a mess their parents have a 'boys will be boys mentality'. They don't expect much of their boys and not in an ugly way, but in a way that allows them to grow up without any expectation. Many girls grow up with the expectation of being perfect angels and they try to live up to that their whole lives. This is essentially the root of the problem and yes, we may not be able to change our childhoods, but we can start to change our mentalities from now; that is what will carry us into the future and allow us to be strong women not good girls.

Women need to learn how to become strong. We hear the term strong woman thrown around a lot in today's culture. Everyone wants to be a strong woman and in fact, everyone thinks they are one. The truth is, not many are. It takes work and a whole mindset change to be a strong woman. If you are stuck in a good girl mindset then there are a few things that you can do to help you along your journey to becoming a strong woman.

The first thing you should do is learn to speak up. Many women do not speak up and just let life pass them by, accepting the things that come their way without ever making their opinions known. You have an opinion and something to say that will add value, not only to your life, but to other people as well. Let your voice be heard and don't be scared of stepping on people's toes. In this day and age, people are so easily offended that it really doesn't matter what you say or don't say, someone will take it the wrong way. It is better to just speak up.

When you do not speak up, you allow people to steamroll you and they will always get what they want, and you will never get what you want. This may lead to you being seriously unhappy in the long run. Decide how you want to live and then ask for it. People can't read your mind, so that is why you have to be vocal. If you think you deserve something then ask for it, if you think someone is disrespecting you or being rude then say something about it.

In the same vein of speaking up, is saying no. If someone asks for something or wants help, you are allowed to say no. Of course, it is good to be there for people and help out where you can but this should never be at the expense of yourself and your needs, otherwise it could lead to burn out. Sometimes, just not wanting to do something is a good enough reason to say no. You know yourself and how much you are capable of giving, be honest and choose to put yourself first.

Remember to stand your ground. Everyone has a certain set of values that they abide by and that direct their lives. You probably know what yours are and you probably have different ones for family, friends, work, etc. If you know what these values are, then stand up for them and as soon as someone tries to overstep their boundaries cut them off right there.

It is ok to stand your ground and refuse to do or say something you think is going against what you believe in or what you want. Be bold and thank people for their input but you really don't have to listen to them. It's great that they want to give you advice, or tell you what they think is right, but it isn't their life. It's yours so take ownership for it and don't let people sway you into their way of thinking.

The next step in ditching the good girl complex is to leave behind the idea of perfection. Perfection is the thing all good girls strive towards. Honestly this is an unmeetable standard if this is what you are reaching for. We are all born imperfect and that's the way we will live out the rest of our lives. We are human and we make mistakes and mess up all the time. Sure, we will learn and grow but that does mean that one day we will be perfect. It is exhausting to keep trying to get something that you will never be able to reach. Now, I'm not saying don't better yourself; do that. Take the opportunities to learn and become a better you, but also set realistic goals. Goals that you will be able to reach and be motivated to do so, then when you reach them you will be motivated for the next one. You can be a great and successful person without being perfect.

Next, learn to be a little selfish if you want to truly

leave behind the stigma of a good girl. Many women may struggle with this because being selfish can be taken the wrong way. When I say selfish, I do not mean meeting your needs at the expense of others, that is wrong. What I do mean is take care of yourself first. Allow yourself the time you need to rest and relax. You don't need to answer to anyone about your life, it's yours to do with as you please.

When we focus too much on other people, we become people pleasers and we are constantly trying to get into someone else's good books. This means that we are at the mercy of another person and our identity is found in what others think of us. Don't give others that power, rather give yourself that power. What do you think about yourself? Does doing this or that make you happy?

Take care of yourself. In this messy world you are the only person who can be trusted to have your best interests at heart 100% of the time. Listen to yourself first before you go out and give of yourself to other people.

The reason the good girl complex is so prevalent in the female mind is mainly because of fear. Fear that we won't be liked. Fear that we are not good enough. Fear that we will offend someone. Fear that we won't be loved. This fear holds us back.

The truth is that if we are truly ourselves then there will be some people who will not like us, and we might have to risk rejection from those people. But be honest, did you like every person you have come across? It's impossible to get along with everyone, there are so many people and personalities out there we can't all possibly just gel together without any tension.

The fear that you are holding onto is unnecessary and it is making you compromise. Once you are just honest about who you are and what you want, then people who are similar and want similar things will be attracted to you. How much better would it be to have a few people around you that you love and that share your interests and values rather than having a big group of people who you have to keep changing for in order to keep them happy? Think about that and decide if holding onto your fear is actually worth your happiness.

With all this being said, treat others well and with respect. Being a strong woman is not about bulldozing people to get what you want. It is about taking care of yourself and then, with the energy you have left, taking care of those around you. Remember you still need people in your life so never isolate yourself under the guise of taking care of yourself. Make yourself the priority but make room for others in your life.

Treat people the way you want to be treated. You can even say no and stand up for yourself in a way that is respectful and kind. When we are considerate, other people will pick up on that and be considerate to us as well. We will always get what we give.

5

Gain Control of Your Emotions and Relationships

Emotions can be our best friend or our worst enemy. We all need to take control of our emotions otherwise they will overtake us and run our lives. Once we learn that our lives are our own and that means that it is ours to make something of or let someone else shape, we will understand how important it is to not be passive but rather take ownership of our own lives and relationships.

Be Your Own Boss

Being your own boss is about taking control of your own life and not letting others control you or make decisions for you. You should have the power to control your own life and make it what you want it. This doesn't mean that you are overly aggressive but rather understanding your own rules for your life and then sticking to them.

A boss does not compromise when it comes to doing what is best for her company. She works hard and doesn't let the opinions of others sway her in every direction, she is steadfast and makes a plan and then gives it all she's got. She understands that there are people under her that are counting on her because her success is ultimately their success and her failure is their failure. As much as people can help her in tough situations, nobody can run her business for her. This is the same for our lives; we are the boss and our lives are our company. People will be counting on us whether we know it or not, so it's up to us to make our lives a success. Even if not for other people, our lives belong to us, so we need to work to make our lives what we want it to be.

When we realize that we are our own bosses we take the bull by the horns and are more open to new opportunities. We have the freedom to say yes to what gives us life and no to the things that drain us. We will feel more fulfilled, more in control and more ready for whatever may come our way. It gives us the confidence to build the life we want and not settle for something lesser, so when a man does come into our lives and wants to change us, or he is not up to the standard that is good for us, we will be able to stand our ground and say no instead of just being swept away.

Bosses own something and when we decide to be our own boss, we take ownership of our own lives. When we take ownership for ourselves, we believe and do what is best for ourselves.

Boundaries

Setting boundaries is something women are notoriously bad at. Many women feel if they set boundaries that they will be pushing people away and that others will find someone else who is willing to bend. This is not true and even if it were, being in a relationship where you are the one that always has to compromise for fear of the other person leaving is not fair or healthy. Both parties need to have boundaries that are set in place even before dating begins. Know what's best for you and what you are willing to compromise on and what you are not.

When it comes to boundaries, it can be difficult to tell what is too much and what is actually beneficial to you and the relationship, especially if you don't have experience with setting them. I want to help with that and give some pointers on how to go about setting and sticking to your boundaries.

It's all well and good to say you want to set boundaries but how you go about doing that will be crucial to the follow through. Boundaries are not something we can make up on the spot or just quickly jot down. It will take some time to figure out what boundaries are right for you and then how to enforce them.

Remember to check in with yourself. How we feel and how our bodies react to certain situations is a good indicator of what boundaries we should be setting. If doing something or being with someone makes you feel uncomfortable or makes you put your guard up, then it's probably because you need to be weary of the situation. Even if someone asks you to do something and you are instantly filled with a feeling of dread or unwillingness, then you need to check why this is as it may not be what is best for you.

Your body signals are also a good indicator of how you are feeling. Sometimes we don't always recognize our feelings, but we can recognize our bodies. If we cross our arms or tense up in a certain situation, it means that we are on our guard and not comfortable with the situation. If we are relaxed, smiling and have open arms that means we are happy and comfortable with the situation.

Our bodies will naturally give us these indicators, but it is our duty to find out why we are reacting this way. Ask yourself, "What about this situation is making me tense/anxious/comfortable/happy?". Really take some time to think. Write it down and the next time you feel the same way make a note of it as well. This way you will be able to track what usually makes you feel certain ways. When you identify what makes you react negatively, you will be able to put up boundaries to prevent those situations from coming up again.

Recognize that only you can truly understand your needs. Everybody has needs, whether they are emotional, physical or spiritual. Not only that, people have different needs from one another. The thing is that nobody will understand your needs the way you do. In this process of setting boundaries, you must learn to understand yourself and what your specific needs are.

Some people are more extroverted and crave human contact to feel energized and loved while others may be more introverted, which means they need time to themselves. Some people are very physical, and love being touched and held, where others feel more loved when someone does something for them, spends time with them, or just has a conversation with them. There are many different ways our love tank can be filled but yours will not be the same as the next person's, so don't look at how other people are in relationships or what Sally's boyfriend does for her. You may just be different and that is why you need to focus this journey inwardly and outwardly.

Ask yourself what do I appreciate and what do I *need* to feel loved. If you are finding it tough to find the answers, then maybe think of what you do for others when you want to appreciate them and make them feel loved. We usually give what we want to get and it is usually easier to pick up what we do for others than what we need for ourselves. Just remember that some of these will be wanted and some of them will be needed and you must sift through these to make sure you know which is which.

A crucial step in setting boundaries is to communicate them to others. It's all well and good to have boundaries but if you keep them to yourself then they will serve no purpose. Once you have made your boundaries and understand what you need you need to communicate them to the people around you, that way they will know what you expect. If others don't know what your boundaries are you can't expect them to respect them.

Now you don't have to write out the list and sick it to your back so people will know your boundaries. Communication can happen in subtle ways and by the way you handle situations. If you are in a new relationship with someone then it may be worth your while to have a conversation with them at some point down the line about what you expect, how you want to be treated, and what is unacceptable for you. These types of conversations do not have to happen often unless there has been constant stepping over boundaries but in this case, you may have to take a second look at the relationship.

In most cases, these conversations may not need to happen as you can communicate your boundaries by what you accept and how you react to certain situations. If you do not like something then don't stand there and watch it happen; feel free to leave or say this topic or situation does not make me feel comfortable and most likely it will change and people will be more conscious next time around. Similarly, if you don't want to be spoken to in a certain way or whatever it may be, just set the boundary down as the situation happens. This is much more effective than laying all your boundaries down at once. It will be too much for the person to take in. If there is a situation and then a boundary set down, men will be more likely to remember it.

Now you know how to set boundaries but what exactly are your boundaries? What areas in your life do you have to set boundaries in? Remember your life has many facets. and there will be different boundaries and expectations for each. We will be discussing a few important areas where boundaries must be set in order to have a healthy and thriving relationship. These are the ones that have to be talked about since they are the most important boundaries in your life.

Expectations are a big one. Many relationships fail because expectations were not managed correctly, or they were not discussed. If two parties in a relationship have different expectations, they will be moving towards two different goals and down the line it will make being together and making decisions very difficult. Let's say you want to get married one day and he does not, if you have never discussed this expectation then he will be living a more chilled lifestyle, never thinking about the long term where you will be thinking about settling down and having a family. Down the line this will either end up with one of you compromising something very important and ultimately being really unhappy or you will have to break up. This is why laying out your expectations at the beginning is so important.

This is a conversation that needs to take place at the beginning of the relationship so that both of you are clear on what each of you wants. When the expectations are laid out it is important for the both of you to be completely honest so that you will be moving forward knowing exactly where the relationship is going. If one of you decides that you are unable to live up or commit to the other's expectations then maybe you need to re-look at the relationship, it may not be right for you and that's ok. Better to know sooner than later.

When setting boundaries, make sure you discuss the

other relationships in your life. Yes, your relationship with your significant other will be the most important to you and it will take up more time than the other relationships in your life, but the fact is that you still have other relationships. All relationships take work, and all are important for a balanced life. Your family and your friends still need you to spend time with them. Remember that all relationships take time so if you do not spend time with someone your relationship will suffer.

If your relationship with your significant other is taking up all your time and you are unable to see other important people in your life then you will have to take a look at how you can set boundaries to curb this issue. Speak to your significant other and tell him that you need to have some time to spend with other people and he should have his own relationships outside of yours as well. Being in an all-consuming relationship may seem romantic for a short while, but eventually you will come to realize it is not healthy or sustainable. Have a chat about the other relationships in your life at the beginning of your relationship, and make sure that both of you understand that even though you really like spending time with one another, there are other relationships that will need your attention.

The next thing you should set boundaries on is your time. Time is our most valuable commodity and it allows us the space to work on ourselves and reach our dreams.

Sometimes we can get so caught up in a relationship that we spend all that time with that person and forget to take time to work on ourselves and just spend time with ourselves. Be intentional about setting aside time for yourself and other things. A relationship should never take you away from the things that you are passionate about, but rather give you someone to support you in the things that you are passionate about.

Set boundaries with your time by making yourself a priority in your own life. If you want to pursue a new skill or a hobby, then do so. Speak to your significant other about it and say that this space is mine and I am going to be practicing this skill, studying this subject or just spending some time with myself. He should have his own hobbies and passions as well. If the time you spend apart is fulfilling than the time you spend together will be that much more magical.

Lastly, you need to set boundaries in terms of your dreams and goals. This is an extremely important one and for the most part cannot be compromised on. When you set dreams and goals, you are setting an outline for your life. It's a guide to where you want your life to head. If you compromise on this that means you are allowing your life to be led in a different direction from what you desire, and think is best for you.

If your partner has different dreams and goals for his life in terms of career path and things similar, these things can be worked around. You don't have to have the exact same dreams and goals, but they need to be able to fit into the general outline of what you want your life to look like. So, if he is an accountant and you are pursuing a career as a lawyer then that shouldn't cause any conflict. However if he wants to immigrate out of the country and that is something you don't see yourself doing because you dream of building a life where you are, then that is something that will cause a problem down the line.

When it comes to big things don't go in hoping that he will change his mind because you don't want to change yours; why expect that from him? Also remember when it comes to dreams and goals the outline has to be aligned but the things that make up what is going on in between does not really hold that much weight, those can be shifted and compromised on.

Once you've set your boundaries and you know what they are (depending if you are in a relationship already, you could have discussed them with your significant other), you now have to action them. It is no good to have boundaries and then let people walk in and out whenever they please.

If you do choose to have a conversation with the people around you who will be affected by setting boundaries, then they should now be aware of what you will tolerate going forward, but remember people will forget so if someone oversteps then you have to make it known. Please don't think that that means being rude or over-assertive about it. Just state that these are your boundaries or that you are not comfortable with something so it's their choice whether they want to respect that or not. If they choose not to respect it then you can choose to leave the situation and even the relationship if it comes to that.

There are some people who are naturally boundary pushers, so they will test how far you are willing to let them go. It is your job to make sure that you don't bend no matter how hard they push. Eventually they will give up and get bored, move on and find someone else to push. This honestly does not make them bad people; they just have this type of personality but remember that you have power to resist as well. Once you have proven that your boundaries are set in stone, there will be very few people that will force things onto you. However, people are people so they may need a reminder every once in a while, so don't get annoyed at this. People usually don't have others on their mind 24/7, even if it is someone they love or are in a relationship with.

It will definitely be hard at the beginning since it is new for you and the people around you, but it has to be done if you expect to live a fulfilling life that does not consist of you being the one to bend for everyone else. Boundaries are a way of telling yourself that you matter, and nobody can take that away from you. You can also decide who is allowed within certain boundaries, this makes sure that it's not any person that is let into your innermost parts.

Boundaries don't mean you will always be saying no. It is actually the opposite; it gives you the freedom to say yes to the things that really matter to you. Boundaries are not used to shut people out but rather to let the right people in, if you think about it in this way you won't feel guilty about saying no to something or someone. Action your boundaries and see how much more freedom you have.

This may not be easy to hear but it is a fact, there will be repercussions to setting boundaries. Some are good and some may feel as though they are bad. Be assured that the ones that feel bad in the moment will actually be for your benefit in the long run.

The truth is that as soon as you put up boundaries, some people will not like it and it may even cause them to walk out of your life. You may see male suitors not making it as far with you as they used to. Think about it, is this really a bad thing? It may feel bad in the moment and feel like people are leaving, but do you really want those people in your life? People that have no respect for your boundaries? The answer should be no. Even if it hurts a little in the beginning there is a bigger picture.

People who have the same expectations, outlook, and outline for their lives will be drawn to you. You will then have more space to let them in. That is the bigger picture, the right people will be able to find you and you will have the freedom to entertain them and see where your relationship could go with them, instead of wasting your time with the wrong people.

Be brave through this process. Don't be afraid to let go of some people. They will find their way back to you if they are meant to, but if not then you have other relationships that need your attention.

Stand Your Ground

It is important to stand your ground in any situation otherwise you run the risk of being run over. Men are naturally boundary pushers so they will always try and see how far they can push; they want their way at the end of the day. This doesn't mean he doesn't care or isn't thinking of you, this is just how people are. We all want what is best and easiest for ourselves and if someone else is willing to bend for us then chances are, we will let them. That is why it is your job to stand up for yourself, both in romantic relationships and in life in general.

I know many women struggle to stand their ground because they think if they do, they will come across as assertive or masculine, but I think that is because there is the wrong view around being assertive. Being assertive is having your say and making sure others around you understand why you don't like something or don't want to do something.

There is a right way and a wrong way to be assertive. Being loud, demeaning and bossy is not being assertive. That is being domineering and nobody likes someone like that. When you are assertive you should still respect the people around you. As soon as you come across as attacking then people will want to defend themselves and attack back, and where does that leave you? With two upset people who are not respectful of each other and there was no decision reached.

The right way to be assertive is to be clear, confident, and considerate of the other person's stand or point. There should be no accusations flying around, words such as "you always" and "you never" shouldn't be used when stating your point. The most effective way to assert yourself is to follow this formula:

1. Start with "When you..." - This phrase highlights one point and one thing that he did, it is not attacking his entire character, morals or values. Focusing on one situation will give him a reference rather than just saying, "You are always like this". Stick to the facts and state what actually happened, don't add in anything extra.
2. Next is "I feel..." - This is focused on how the behavior or action made you feel. You are not making your feelings his problem but rather helping him understand that what he did or said had an effect on you.

3. State the "Because..." - This shows how his actions have affected you. Pick something that is easily observable, not something general.

4. End with "I want..." - This is where you make your request for a change in behavior. State what you would like to change in the situation, make sure you pick one thing that is specific to the situation you are talking about. Being too general means that he won't know what you want him to change. If there is nothing for him to do so he most likely won't change anything at all.

The statement should sound something like:

"When you invited your friends over without asking me, I felt disrespected, because people were invited into my space without my consent and I had to change what I was doing to accommodate them. I would like you to consult me before inviting people over to our house in future."

Do you see how much better that sounds rather than "Your friends are always at our house and I have no space for myself!". Anger and emotional outbursts will get you nowhere. Clear statements make it easy to see the problem and give direction on how to fix it. Remember that men are natural fixers so if you don't give them a way to fix the situation then they are likely to not do anything at all.

Always remember that you are allowed to say no

whenever you feel like something is not right or you are not comfortable, however don't make *no* your first reaction. When someone asks for something from you always consider their request first. Make sure you are saying no because of something valid rather than just because. You will need people just as much as they need you, so don't burn your bridges.

You need to choose when to say no and when to say yes. After you have thought about the request and come to the conclusion that it is not for you, you are then allowed to say no. Be tactful and state your opinion. You don't necessarily have to give the reason for why you are saying no but it does help to give some context. If you don't have the time then say so, if you are too tired then state that, if you are very busy at the moment make it known. People appreciate and are more understanding if the *no* is accompanied by a small reason, even if it is general.

There are a few things that you should stand your ground on. We are going to take a look at these things and talk through ways in which you can practically stand your ground in each respective situation.

Firstly, let's talk about finances. This is a big thing and if you will eventually be sharing bills and merging assets then it is something that you will have to talk about and make sure you are on the same page. One person cannot make all the decisions and it does not matter who earns more, you will be partnering together.

Address this as a concern if your man has all the financial power and you don't get to be part of the decisions. Budget and plan so both of you know where the money is going and are aware of what you can spend and what you cannot. Any big purchases or financial decisions need to be discussed and agreed upon.

Privacy is definitely something you need to stand your ground on. Even though you two are a couple now, you need to have space and privacy. If he is a very controlling person that wants all your passwords and login details, this can be a problem and you have every right to say no. Explain that you have nothing to hide but you do not have to let him into your social media or whatever else in order to prove that. In the same way, you should not expect him to give you his passwords, rather not even ask. If either of you willingly gives the other their logins, then that is a different story but don't let that be an expectation.

You should also know how fast or slow you want the relationship to go and stand firm on that. There is a pace that you should be comfortable with when it comes to your relationship and it should be expressed. This goes hand in hand with setting expectations. As soon as you start feeling uncomfortable with the pace of the relationship then have a conversation about it.

Sometimes at the beginning of the relationship we are in the honeymoon phase and it just feels like things are moving at lightning speed. You are talking about your future together, kids, a house and all of that but there may be a point when you or he realizes that you're moving too fast. Talk about slowing things down, if you need more time to get to know each other a bit more before making any major decisions then that is a perfectly reasonable request.

If you feel like the relationship is moving too slow and you are not progressing towards settling down, then you should also bring this up. Ask the important questions like do you guys see this relationship ending in marriage? Is marriage something you want? Stand your ground when it comes to this because if he doesn't want to get married and it is something you desire then neither of you should change your mind on something so big, otherwise one of you will be very unhappy down the line. Have these conversations, they are very important to both of your happiness.

Now with all these things that you should not compromise on, there are actually a few that you should be able to be flexible with. Small things can definitely be compromised on. Not everything has to be a struggle or a big fight, relationships are about compromise. The more you compromise on the certain things the more inclined he will be to make compromises for you.

Things that you should compromise on are:

- What to eat - Allow him to choose where to eat as well. You may not have the same taste, but it really won't kill you to eat the foods that he likes once in a while.

- Home decor - If you both share the home then what goes in it needs to be a shared decision.

- Friends & family - Let him have time to share with the other people in his life. Allow him the space to have other relationships.

- Activities - You probably won't have all the same interests so spend some time doing what the other person wants to do. Watch his favorite shows, learn about his favorite sport or activity. He will definitely appreciate it, but don't overdo this or it will be evident that you did it.

Having a Healthy Relationship

The reason there are so many men who are unhappy in relationships and try to find a way out is because they feel like they are being held down and caged. Nobody wants to feel caged and like they aren't able to think for themselves. That isn't a relationship, that is jail. Nobody wants to be in a jail cell, so we don't want our men to feel like we are a jail cell.

Women are naturally nurturing and that is a wonderful quality but sometimes we can take it too far. We become 'helicopter parents' but to our significant other. No man wants a controlling woman. It is in fact one of the biggest peeves of the straight, male population; it is where the expression 'the old ball and chain' came from. Men feel like they are being chained to their woman and that means they look at her as an obligation not someone they love and enjoy spending time with.

The only way to have a healthy relationship is to let him go. Let him experience his life and make the mistakes he needs to. Your function is not to guide him, protect him or make decisions for him. Your job is to support him, to love him and to help him up when he falls down. But you have to let him fall down. He is a grown up and he has his own life to live so let him be a grown up, let him decide how he wants his life to play out.

Remember that you are not his mom and you don't want to be. A helicopter parent is a parent that follows their child around and makes sure they are ok all the time. When something goes wrong, they are there to defend, protect and comfort their child. No matter where the child goes the parent is always there to give them advice and to solve their problems. Now, as much as this may sound like a caring parent, this is an unhealthy relationship for parent and child. The child never learns to do anything for themselves, they become lazy since all the decision making is not theirs and they become resentful of their parents down the line. Now if this is true for parenting then it is even more so when we are in an adult relationship with a man.

Can you imagine having someone hovering around you saying, "do this," "do that," "not like that," "I'll do it for you!" It is so annoying, and it can actually be suffocating. Every time he turns around you are there offering him solutions, input and 'a better way to do it'. Leave that man alone, he is a grown man and you are not his mother! He needs your support not your mothering. He already has a mother and he has passed the stage in his life where he needs her to do everything for him, so he doesn't need someone to replace her.

As we have stated before, you are dating or want to date a full-grown man not a baby and a full-grown man is responsible for his own life. If you don't allow him the space to do so, then he never will and there are two scenarios here:

1. He will end up resenting all your input. He will be frustrated and start rebelling; he won't come to you or tell you what he is doing because he doesn't want your opinion. This leaves you with a man that doesn't speak to you and doesn't enjoy spending time with you.
2. He will let you take control of his life, then he will become lazy. He won't know how to make decisions and will always rely on you for everything. Down the line this will put a strain on

your relationship because in the long term you will be unable to carry both of you. Everything will rest on you and he will become the shell of the man he used to be and both of you will be frustrated.

Both of these scenarios are horrible, and I'd bet that no woman wants this in their men. That is why it is crucial to let him take control of his own life and make his own decisions. The fact is that he made it this long without your help, so he is capable of making his own decisions and being in control of his own life.

Remember that you are still your own person and if you spend so much time trying to control his life you will never focus on yourself. Both of you need to develop the ability to work on yourselves, develop your own skills and talents. If you give him the space to work on himself and you have the space to work on yourself, now you have two people who are there to support each other but still take ownership of themselves.

Focus on your health, exercise, join a club, do something that you love. When you do this, you become an interesting person. You have things to talk about other than your significant other and spending this time apart will actually make you more attractive to him. Absence does make the heart grow fonder and it makes you get better.

A common question when speaking about leaving

men to do their own thing is, "How do I support him if I leave him alone or don't offer my opinion?" The answer to this is found in the difference between emotional support and informational support.

Informational support is when he comes across a problem or challenge and you give your opinion or give him a strategy to get out of it. You are providing him with information to beat the challenge or resolve the problem. Emotional support is when he faces that problem or challenge and you are there for him but the words you speak are encouraging him to figure it out for himself. Saying things like, "You've got this" or "Whatever you end up doing, I will support you." Being there for them if it doesn't work out and celebrating with them when it does.

Emotional support is what men need not informational support. When you support them emotionally it gives them the strength and the confidence to do it themselves. They become better and stronger people knowing that you are there for them but are not controlling them. Every man wants to feel like a man, he wants to be able to fix things and take control. As soon as you offer information he feels as though you are taking that away from him but when you support him emotionally, he gains the strength he needs to be the best he can be.

In order to have that healthy relationship, you need to be able to let him go. A relationship should feel free and give you a sense of happiness when you are in it. You are supposed to feel lighter and more capable when you are with the right person. So, if your man feels weighed down and stuck, he is not going to be happy and as a result you are not going to be happy.

As women we need to learn how to let men go, let him make his own mistakes and then learn from them. Don't always be trying to solve his problems and make his life easy, you are training him to be dependent and that is not good for either of you.

True love is allowing people to become the best version of themselves, not holding onto them so tightly that they don't have the freedom to grow. Freedom is one of our most valued commodities and we resent those that want to take that away. Even if you mean well, don't be someone who takes away someone else's freedom. Instead be the woman that releases him into his full potential. He will always come back to you; he will love you more and respect you more.

6

Guide for Girls Who Are Too Nice - Avoid Being Taken for Granted

Being a nice girl is great, you are soft, kind and caring and all of those are beautiful traits. But unfortunately, because of these traits it is easy to be taken advantage of. There is a saying 'good girls come last' and from what I've seen this can be true.

Now I don't want you to completely change yourself

and become this hard bad-ass girl if it is not your personality, but the reason good girls end up coming out last is because they don't recognize when they are being used and taken advantage of.

Rather than changing everything about yourself, learn to spot people who will use you and avoid them. This way you still get to be who you are but won't be taken advantage of, it's the best way to handle a situation like this.

How to Spot a User

Now it is important to note that not all guys are users. There are some really good guys out there, but the reality is that if you are in the dating scene the chances are you will meet at least one user. It is what it is and not all guys are sent from heaven, unfortunately. Don't get disheartened if you do meet one and don't swear off men and start a "Men Are Trash" Facebook page. Yes, it does suck but if you spot the signs early enough, you will be able to avoid the situation before you get too invested and he gets too lucky.

Like with anything there are signs that will point you to a user. Learn to hone your skills when it comes to recognizing them. At the end of the day if something is making you feel uneasy or something is just not sitting right then you should do a little more investigation, whether it is internally or externally. Find out what is making you feel uneasy and why. Sometimes our bodies and feelings are a little bit ahead of our brains.

There may be signs that are not on this list so feel free to add some more onto your own personal list. These are just the most common and they are the easiest to spot. If your man is only showing one or two of the signs, then it might be worth it to just talk to him about it because he might not even know what he is doing or how it is making you feel. However, if he is showing multiple signs on a consistent basis then you need to be wary of him, he might be in it for the wrong reasons.

Here are some signs to spot a user:

He is selfish. Any healthy relationship is a give and take. Both parties need to be willing to give more than they take, that way both of your needs will be getting met. If you feel like you're the one that is constantly giving and there is little to no giving on his part, then this is a red flag. In fact, this is one of the biggest red flags. Someone who is really interested in being in a relationship will be concerned about the other person and want to care for them and about them, and if this is not happening then you probably have a user on your hands.

Selfishness can take place emotionally, with time and

even sexually. If you feel as though all he wants is what is best for him then it is a problem. He should be concerned about you and what is good for you. If not, then he is selfish and will do whatever it takes to get the best outcome for himself instead of thinking about you.

He is a smooth talker. Smooth talkers always get the ladies and that is exactly why you should be wary of a guy that knows all the right things to say. Smooth talkers have practice with a lot of girls that is why they are able to just know what to say and when to say it. The chances are that you are not the only one he is speaking to and if that is the case then he is not in the relationship for the right reasons.

Everything works on his schedule. Guys who are users want everything their way and on their time. He will only reply to you when he feels like it; of course, you should be understanding if he has a hectic job but if you are only getting texts or calls from him late at night then he could just be looking at you as someone to keep him entertained when he needs it, rather than someone to be in a relationship with.

At the end of the day life does get busy but if a man is really interested in you then he will make the time to see you and talk to you. Only having late night visits from him show you that he really only wants one thing. If that is the case then don't give him sex, wait it out and see if he sticks around. If not, then you saved yourself the trouble of dealing with a person that was only ever interested in you for his own gain.

You haven't met his family or friends. Don't expect him to introduce you to his family in the first week of dating him, these things do take time. Around the three- to six-month marks is an appropriate time to start meeting the people closest to him. If this time has lapsed and you haven't even met his friends, then you may have a problem.

Naturally men want to show off things that they are proud of so if they are happy to be in a relationship with you then they would be showing you off to their friends at the very least. If he hasn't let you into that part of his world, you are probably not that important to him and he doesn't see you as someone that he would want to have a future with. Men love getting approval from their friends, it is a big part of the decision-making process for them so if you haven't met anyone in his world, he definitely isn't thinking long term.

Your friends don't like him. What your friends think is so important when you are in the dating game. They will be able to see things that you can't and will be able to give you different perspectives, plus they only want what is best for you. If you are scared that your friends are out to get you or are always judgy then maybe you need to get some new friends. But for the most part every girl should have friends who they love and trust and these are the friends you should be listening to.

He has a bad reputation. A reputation speaks volumes, it is something that will show his patterns and what other people are thinking about him. Of course if it is just one or two people that are speaking negatively about him then you don't have to listen to that as that could be happening for a few different, explainable reasons but if it is coming from many different people then it would be worth it to see why his reputation is so bad.

People don't just change overnight and even if he has changed you need to be wary of any signs that he might be reverting back to his old ways. A reputation is almost like a history book and it will give you insight into what he was like and what to expect in the future. If his reputation is not good, then you are under no obligation to stick around and see if he will change.

He doesn't show affection. Naturally people will show affection to those they love and value. If there is no affection being shown, then he does not hold you to that standard and has put you in a specific box that he wants to keep at a distance. He might even show you affection but if as soon as you are out in public then he doesn't want to touch you, that is also a red flag. This could mean that he does not want to be seen with you because he has someone else waiting in the wings and doesn't want to get caught.

You are not the only woman he is seeing. If a man is seeing more than one woman then he does not want a relationship; what he wants is as many toys as he can get his hands on. He is not focused on giving time and attention to one woman because he wants to get what he wants from multiple different women. If you ever find out that he is dating other women then you need to ask yourself if you are comfortable with being one of many or if you want to be the only one. My advice would be to value yourself enough to be the only one.

What to Do When You Know He's a User

If your man is showing signs of being a user, the first thing you need to do is have a conversation about it with him. Like I mentioned before, if he is just showing one or two signs then it might just be that he is doing it unknowingly and once you have had the conversation, he will realize it and change. I wouldn't get my hopes up for this scenario because it is a rare ending.

If he is defending himself, saying all the right things and dancing around the issue without giving you a straight answer then he is playing you. He knows he has been caught out and he is just trying to convince you otherwise. Don't be swayed by him, lay down the rules, tell him what you expect from the relationship and if he cannot commit to it then cut him off. He may say that he will change but don't believe him until you see the proof.

If he doesn't change and makes no effort to be different then leave him. It's the only thing you can do otherwise you will be continuously taken for granted. Once you have made up your mind, stick to it and don't let him worm his way back, cut him out. Delete his number, block him and don't allow yourself to fall back into that trap. You are better off without him and now you have the space to meet and date someone who truly respects you.

Actions vs Words

Some men are just sweet talkers, they know exactly what to say and when to say it. When you are angry with them, they know the correct formula to calm you down and when you are upset with them, they know how to make you forgive them. These men are dangerous and are filled with empty promises.

The only way to recognize a man like this is to wait it out and see if his actions match his words. If not, then he is just in it for what he can get, and he is trying to keep you on a string. What this means is that he wants you to come when he says come and stay when he says stay, he wants everything on his terms and knows what to say to get it that way. He may apologize and seem humble but if this is not followed by some sort of action, he didn't mean it.

That is the dangerous thing about words, they sound so good in the moment and so genuine that you almost have to believe them. The thing is that it is not the words that are important, it is the follow up actions that hold the most weight. Words can just be said and forgotten but actions create a lasting memory. Promises are not made just by the initial words; they are made up of the follow-through after the words were said. If there is no follow-through then the words are meaningless, and the promise doesn't exist.

If you notice he is always talking and never doing, then run as fast as you can because your relationship will always be filled with the same scenario. He does something you don't like, he makes empty promises, you forgive him and get your hopes up and then he does it again. If you notice this as a continuous pattern, then it's time to leave. There is only so much you can do; a relationship is about two people and if you can't see eye to eye on important things then it's not worth it. Hold out for someone who will keep his word and do what he says he will. That is the mark of a truly honest person, he keeps to what he says by following through with action.

Treat Yourself the Way You Want Him to Treat You

You can't expect others to treat you like a queen if you don't believe that you are one and treat yourself like a queen. People will only treat you to the level that you put forward and if you think of yourself as lower then that's what people will treat you as. It's not really their fault because they are just following what was modelled to them, in the back of their minds they are thinking, "Oh, this is how she likes to be treated". They don't know any better, but you do. You know that you want to be treated like you are amazing and worth something. If you really believe that then you have to show it in the way you act towards yourself and the way you carry yourself.

Every person has worth, the trick is that other people only see the level of worth that you project outwardly and they will react to that accordingly. It's like a price tag that you put on yourself. When someone sees something they like, the first thing they do is look at the price tag to see if they can afford it. If they can they buy it, take it home and take care of it. If they cannot afford it then they put it back and look for something that they can afford. The same principle applies to us when we show what we are worth on the outside. People who can't afford that or who just don't know how to pay that much will just leave and there will be no wasted time and mismanaged feelings. But the people who can afford you and are willing to give what is required to be in a relationship with you will do so and because the expectations were set from the beginning, everyone is on the same page.

It all starts with respecting yourself, if you don't respect yourself then why should anyone else? When you respect yourself then you won't just drop your standards and settle for whatever is available. You have the right to be picky because you know how much you are worth and are not willing to negotiate. No one walks into a jewelry store and tries to bargain for a diamond; if you cannot afford it then you move onto something else. The jeweler is not worried if the diamond will get sold, he knows it will because it is beautiful and valuable. People only negotiate and bargain for things that are of little value so don't let others convince you that your standards are too high and that you are closing yourself off to opportunity. If you have to lower yourself to get that opportunity, then it isn't worthwhile.

You are in charge of your own life so make it a dynamic one. A dynamic life is one characterized by pursuing your goals and interests, doing things that spark joy into you and continuously trying to grow and have new experiences. If you haven't tried to do something new in a while, then I think it's time that you just pick something and do it. The more dynamic and full your life is, the more interesting people you will meet. You will not meet amazing people by sitting at home knitting, you need to get out there and make your life a life worth living.

Interesting people are attracted to interesting people so if you feel as though there are not enough people around you that are fun and cool then you need to change the places that you hang out and maybe even change your hobbies. In this day and age there is so much to do and so much to see, don't close yourself off to an amazing life because you are too scared to make a change. They say change is as good as a holiday because it shifts your perspective and allows you to think differently, because of this your mind is refreshed.

So, take the leap, try new things and pursue the things that set your soul on fire. In doing so you will meet people that are doing the same thing and those are the people you want to surround yourself with and possibly eventually date.

Remember that insecurity always attracts the wrong guys. When we are insecure, we attract guys who like insecure women. These guys are really not the greatest, the only reason they like insecure women is because it gives them an ego boost. An insecure woman is easy to manipulate and will do anything to keep the man they are with because they are scared, they will not find another. This allows the guy to act however and do whatever he wants with little to no repercussions. He can say whatever he wants knowing that if he works the right angle, she will be the one to apologize. He can make empty promises and treat her how he pleases because she doesn't expect anything more from him.

When we are insecure, we are needy because we feel as though we need a guy to complete us, so when we find a guy that wants to be with us, we cling to him and do everything we can to keep him. This is what leads to women being used and disrespected. We have no need to be insecure when we know how much we are worth. How you see yourself is how others will see you and it will determine what you attract. A guy that wants an insecure woman is probably insecure himself and that is why he wants someone to boost his ego, someone who will do anything to be with him. In this scenario it is best for you both to go and work on yourselves before getting into another relationship.

You need to know yourself before you can get to know someone else. Many people do not take the time to really get to know themselves, what they like or dislike, what they want from life and what they believe in. If you do not know these things about you then you cannot expect someone else to. Once you know yourself then you will know what you like and what you expect. It will make dating and relationships a lot easier.

A good indicator of whether you know yourself or not is when someone asks you to tell them about yourself.

Do you freeze up and not know what to say or do the words come naturally? If you can't describe yourself, then you probably don't know much about yourself. Take the time to figure this out before moving on to find someone to be with. They need to know what they are getting themselves into with you so you should be able to tell them. When you know yourself then it is easier to know what you want and when you know what you want, you won't settle for something lesser just because it is available.

When you know yourself, you will be less hard on yourself and will not be scared to look inwardly and see if maybe you are the root of the problem; you will be more confident in your flaws and your strengths. Someone who is aware of their flaws but does not let that knock their confidence is someone worth being with because they are willing to make the changes and work on themselves and that means that they will be willing to work on the relationship. They are not blinded by a false sense of security or insecurity.

The way you treat yourself will be the way others treat you; you will always set the standard and others will follow. But how do you set the standard? How do you let others know what is acceptable and what is not without being pushy or writing out a long list? The answer is simple really: Treat yourself well first. When you do this, it sets the base for other people to follow. When you value yourself and treat yourself well, you lift the standard of how you expect others to treat you. Once you have mastered treating yourself well then move on to treating others the way you would like to be treated. This is so important. Most people will reciprocate what you do for them because they appreciate it. And when they do something you like, reinforce that behavior by being appreciative of it, the person on the other end will catch on quickly.

7

The Psychology of a Man

It doesn't take a rocket scientist to discover that men and women are very different. Men have a different way of thinking than women and if we try and understand men from our point of view, we will drive ourselves insane. We need to step into the mind of a man and understand how they think from a man's point of view. Once we understand that and recognize the differences females and males have,

we will be in a better position to see what we have been doing that have been particularly annoying for him and why that is so. With that information we can resolve the issue and create a stronger relationship for both parties involved.

Ten Things that Turn a Man Off

Just like there are things that women find unattractive about men, there are many things that women do that men just cannot stand. I will just touch on ten of them, these are the most important and the most common. Once we pinpoint the things that turn men off and then understand why they don't like it, we will be able change it from our side. This is not meant to be an exercise where we change important things about ourselves to fit into a mold of what a man wants, but rather being considerate to how these things make a man feel. In all honesty none of these things are so big that it would cause a woman to drop her standards or morals, so they are easy fixes.

The first thing is having a superiority complex. With the rise of feminism, it seems that there are many women who have mistook the fight for women's rights as putting men down and men are getting tired of it. Part of masculinity is proving yourself and being the alpha male so when a woman (especially one he loves) puts a man down it is a knock to his pride. Just because he is a man does not make him incapable or dumb, it's this stereotyping that women have fought against for so long but are now putting right back onto men. You are both equals, believe that and live that out.

Second, is when you make plans for him. Nothing annoys a man more than when he comes home from a long week at work and all he wants to do is relax or spend some time with the boys but finds out his significant other has already made plans for his weekend without consulting him. Now he is stuck having dinner with your cousins instead of having some downtime with his friends, and you wonder why he has been moody all night. He is his own person and just because you are in a relationship does not give you the right to make plans for him. If you want him to do something with you then ask beforehand and even more importantly, if he says no, then respect that.

The third thing is being oblivious to the little things he does. Men may not express their feelings in a thousand words, there was only one Shakespeare and you are not dating him. They do little things for you to show you that they care. The worst thing for a man is if they are constantly doing little things for you and trying to show you how much they like to or care for you and you just never notice. So if he opens the door for you, say thank you. If he stands up when you walk into the room, acknowledge that. If he makes you a cup of tea before bed, appreciate it. Whatever small thing he does, make sure he knows you notice, and you appreciate him for it.

In that same vein, reciprocate his gestures. Men want to feel loved and taken care of just as much as women do, even if they don't express it. So, show him that you care, be there for him and listen to him and his needs as well.

Number four is being self-centered. Do you know those mean girls from the movies that were so vapid and self-centered, the ones that every girl hated? Well when they exist in real life guys hate them too. A woman that is self-centered is such a turn off to a guy, he wants to care about you more than you care about you. When you are too focused on you then you can't focus on anybody else.

The fifth thing that turns a man off is acting dumb or clumsy. This one stems from the misconception that all men want to do is help women and therefore a woman must be less intelligent than him and completely clumsy in order to attract a man. The funny thing is that women took this and ran with it and that's why we have movies like *Clueless* and *Legally Blonde.* Granted those are great movies, but they are not the type of people we should aspire to be because no man finds that attractive. Men are ultimately looking for a partner, someone they can grow with and who challenges them, not someone to baby or keep catching every time she trips over her own feet.

Sixth on the list is being too judgmental. Let's face it,

us women do have a tendency to be a bit judgmental and most of the time it stems from a place of insecurity, but we can't put others down to make ourselves look good. Making fun of Suzy's new haircut and Betty's mismatched outfit is one of the quickest ways to turn off a guy. Men like a woman who cares for others, not puts others down. Remember the old saying, "If you don't have something nice to say, don't say anything at all". These are words to live by.

Men like to be in the moment so thinking too far into the future is the seventh thing that could turn your man off. Men love savoring the moment and just being present in what is happening now. Women, on the other hand, have a tendency of thinking 500 steps ahead, in some cases this is a good thing, but in others it is not. When you are out celebrating your first anniversary, he is not thinking about celebrating your 40th anniversary with grandkids in a nice house in the suburbs. So, don't bring that up. He wants to enjoy the moment with you instead of thinking about things that haven't happened yet.

It takes a lot for a guy to be open and honest so when he does open up, he does not want your conversation to be shared with your best friend, your sister and your mom, that is why the eighth turn-off is sharing his secrets. He wants to know that he can trust you, so keep it between you two. I'm sure you wouldn't like your innermost thoughts to be shared with a bunch of his friends.

Number nine is purposefully making him jealous. Naturally, men do get a little jealous when other guys are giving you attention and that is ok if you are not purposely going out to talk to other guys just to get a reaction from him. When you do that, it seems as though you do not value the relationship you two have or are insecure about your relationship. A man does not want to feel like he has to fight for your attention or prove himself over and over again, especially if you are already in a relationship with him. Relationships are not a game so take them seriously and respect him.

The tenth and final thing that turns men off is expecting him to read your mind. Sometimes men can be a little clueless to a woman's feelings but if we are going to be honest, we can be clueless when it comes to ourselves as well. So give the guy a break. He does not know how you are feeling or what you want and sometimes he does not know what he did to make you mad. It happens, men are not mind-readers, so if you are upset or angry tell him why. If you want something then don't make him guess, just be straightforward instead of leaving the poor guy to wrack his brain the whole night trying to figure you out.

How to Communicate Effectively

Men and women are so different from each other, sometimes us being attracted to the opposite sex seems like a cruel joke. The way men and women think, speak, and act differ greatly from each other, there is no doubt about that, but with that being said there are ways to communicate effectively with each other.

Communication is the foundation of any healthy relationship; we just need to figure out how to make it work for us and how to meld the two different types of communication together. But before we are able to do that, it is so important to understand the differences between men and women when it comes to how we communicate and how we use communication.

For men communication and talking is to reach an objective, it's a means to an end. They use it to make plans and state problems that need to be fixed. Even when he is speaking to his friends there is a point to be made, that is why we see many men having these friendly debates. They all want to state their point and prove why they are right.

Men usually sort through everything in their heads

before they speak it out loud. They are inward processors and once they know what they want to say, that is when they will say it. It is all about efficiency and the delivery. This is why men draw into themselves when something is wrong; they choose not to speak about what is going on because they have to figure it out for themselves first. Once they have wrapped their heads around it or have developed some sort of plan or have found the solution, they will happily share it with you.

When he is listening, he is listening with the intent to fix or solve whatever problem is presented. Listening is not a passive exercise; it must always lead to some sort of result. Once he has listened, the next step is to solve the problem and give you the solution. That is how a man's brain is wired even though it may not make much sense to us women.

On the other hand, a woman's communication style is completely different to a man's. She speaks to feel better and to bond with the people around her. The main focus of communication to a woman is to create and build relationships, that is why women can talk for hours on end about the most random subjects. Talking, for a woman, is a way to release everything she is holding onto and in the process, she discovers how she is feeling and that brings her closer to the person she is talking to.

Where men are inward thinkers, women are outward thinkers. For a woman everything needs to be out of her head before she is able to sort through it. That is why women need someone to just listen because they will sort through their own mess as long as they have a sounding board to direct the words to. You will notice that when a woman is venting, the woman she is speaking to will hardly say anything besides a few agreeing or encouraging words but by the end of the conversation the woman that was venting feels a lot better and has resolved the situation. This is just how women process things.

For a woman a conversation has its own value, it is not a vehicle to get somewhere else. When she enters into a conversation, she is not thinking about what she will get out of it or how she will answer any coming questions, she just enjoys the time she has in the conversation.

We need to learn how to bridge the gap, the reason men and women find it so hard to communicate is because men want to talk to women as they do men and vice versa. At the end of the day each party aims to do what is best for the other but the problem is that men think that what a woman wants is the same thing as a man and women think a man wants the same thing as a woman. Can you see how this becomes a problem? Men cannot talk to women as one of the boys because she will not respond to it in the same way because her needs are different. In the same way a man's needs cannot be met in the same way as one of the girls. We need to change our strategy if we want to be able to communicate effectively with the opposite sex.

Be cognizant of the fact that your man has different

needs when it comes to communication. Don't be offended when he doesn't react the same as your girlfriends when you just want him to talk, respect his need for space. He will come to you when he is ready to talk. He isn't trying to keep something from you, he is trying to process internally first.

Remember that all people are not the same, so even though men and women have these general categories that they fall into there will be some differences with each person. If you are confused about something, then ask. Ask your man how he would like you to support him or communicate with him. Speak about what your needs are and what his are. When you have a better understanding of each other, it will result in a lot less frustration and hurt feelings. Remember to have grace for each other, communication is a messy thing and you won't always get it right but always keep trying.

How to Tell if He Likes You

Men are confusing creatures; they act so different to us and still we find ourselves drawn to them. The question of whether he likes you or not has been asked by many women and it is a scenario that causes women to wrack their brains and still end up with no answer.

Figuring out if a man likes you can seem like an impossible task but there are signals and signs that you can pick up on to help you discover whether he likes you. However, it is important to note that every man is different and just because he does not show all of these signs does not mean that he does not like you. He may show all of them but then again, he may only show one or two. This is just a guide to help you pick up on the signs that you may have otherwise overlooked.

Check his body language. Guys may not be big talkers, but they do use their body language a great deal. You can always tell how someone is feeling by checking their body language. Is he turned towards you and leaning in when you talk? Is his body open, meaning his arms are relaxed and his feet pointed to you? These are all positive signs that he is interested in you.

Another good sign is if he moves things out of the way to make sure there is nothing between you two. When someone is uncomfortable, they put up a barrier either with objects or by crossing their arms and being closed off. So if he is open, relaxed and there are no objects between you, then these are all indicating that he is interested in you.

Does he get shy around you? This could be a sign that he likes you. Guys usually like to portray themselves as strong and outgoing but sometimes when they are with a girl that they like they get a bit nervous and can end up being shy. They will lose their train of thought and stutter and may even tell a few lame jokes to try and hide it. If he is nervous or shy around you then you definitely have some sort of effect on him.

In a crowded room does he find you? When you are in a group does he make more of an effort to talk to you or stand next to you? We are naturally drawn to the people we like; we want to be in their presence and spend time with them. Guys are no different. If he puts down his phone when he is speaking to you it shows that he is eliminating distractions and wants to be fully present with you. Giving you his full attention is definitely a good sign.

Just in case you didn't know already, men are naturally turned on by touch. They are physical by nature so if he finds ways to touch you (innocently or not) then he probably has a thing for you. He may put his hand on the small of your back to guide you somewhere or remove something stuck in your hair or clothing. However silly the reason, he will find a way to initiate physical contact.

If a man acts a little goofy when he is around you it is a good sign. Acting goofy around you means he is letting his guard down and allowing you to see his quirky, silly side. He may tease you a bit and make silly comments to get you to laugh. Guys love to make women laugh so go along with it, tease back. It will make him smile and give him the indication that you are ok with being a bit silly around him as well.

One of the most obvious signs that he is into you is if

he compliments you. This is a simple one, he wouldn't be complimenting you if he didn't like you. Men are not like women who will just compliment anyone about anything. They are quite selective so know if he is complimenting you then he really means it. If he does give you a compliment, accept it with a smile, let him know that you appreciate it.

Another common sign is that he remembers what you said and asks questions. A guy that likes you will remember things that you said in past conversations and bring them up again. This shows that he was paying attention to what you said and that your conversations matter to him. He will also ask you questions; he wants to find out about you and doesn't only want to talk about himself. When a man finds a woman intriguing, he wants to find out more so he will be curious to find out more.

If you are still unsure then his friends are a good indicator of how he feels about you. Do they leave you alone when you two start talking? That means that they sense that there is something between you. Do they make jokes about you and him? That means he has been talking to them about you. Guys love to tease their friends when they like someone, it's just part of what boys do. Any kind of similar behavior from his friends indicates that he has been mentioning you to his friends and when a man starts talking about a woman to other people it's a sure sign that he likes her.

How to React to His Signals

There are a few things you can do to react to the signals he is laying down. Remember flirting is a two-way street, he is doing all of this to get your attention and see if you like him as well. Make sure you clearly show him that you are interested in him; that will boost his confidence and you will end up with the result you wanted much quicker.

You can also make the first move here; some guys are on the shyer side and will feel more comfortable making a move knowing that you are showing some interest in him. Don't be afraid to flirt a little and show your cheeky side, men love the attention and it will open the door for him to start leading after he is more certain that you are interested in him.

If he is flirting with you or showing any of the above signs, then the best thing to do is just be playful. Guys love being teased and love a girl who can joke around. In a cute manner make fun of something he is wearing or the way he says something. Remember guys are physical so when you are doing this try and get in a sneaky touch as well. An arm rub, light punch or a shoulder squeeze go a long way for a man.

Also, men love to be complimented just as much as women, just make sure you are complimenting the right things. Men like to be complimented on what they do rather than what they look like. So find an excuse for him to do something, ask him to open a bottle, reach something you can't or whatever else you can think of and then compliment him on how helpful he was and be genuine about it. Men love to feel needed; this is the type of compliment that works best for them.

Lastly whatever they do, try to reciprocate. He touches you, you touch him. He gives you attention, you give him attention. He compliments you, you compliment him. Now you don't have to do it directly after he does it for you. Wait a bit but make sure he knows that you have the same feelings for him as he does for you and his advances are not going unnoticed.

Conclusion

Life isn't about finding the right person to complete you, it is about being the very best version of yourself. Where so many women go wrong is that they spend so much time focusing on trying to find the perfect man that they forget to become a worthwhile woman. A man can never fill an empty space, he has his own things to deal with and it is unfair to put that kind of pressure on someone. If you can't find contentment and happiness with yourself, then why would it be ok to saddle someone else with that responsibility?

Take the time to get to know yourself, know your likes and dislikes. Find out what sparks a fire in you and see what you want to pursue. Believe in yourself and do your best to reach your dreams. These are all things that someone who finds herself valuable will be striving for. The great thing is that when you do this, when you become your own person, you become dynamic and the right men will find you. It will be easier to say no to the type of men that will use you and the type of men that are not willing to put in the effort in the relationship. If you know your worth then others will see that and you won't have to drop your standards, others will raise theirs.

Men are completely different to women so take the time to understand them. Practice communication and think about the things that he likes. If you are in a relationship with a man already then make sure you are finding out about him specifically. As much as there is a general blueprint for men, it is only a guideline and you have to make the effort to make the relationship work. Getting the man is only a small portion of the journey, creating a worthwhile and fulfilling relationship is significantly harder but the rewards are great.

The tips and tricks we have gone over in this book will allow you to navigate the male mind and the dating world with more ease. Whenever there are people and emotions involved it will be a bit messy so there is no exact step-by-step guide but having this blueprint to help guide you will be a great benefit to you. Remember that you can always page back and review a section that you need depending on what you are struggling with and what stage of the dating process you are in.

The most important thing to remember about dating is to have fun. Many women get so much into their heads that they miss the magic of dating and being in a relationship. The truth is that we will all embarrass ourselves and maybe we will say something wrong and scare the guy off, that's ok you can just try again. It's not the end of the world. Learn to laugh at yourself and not overthink, most things will flow naturally if you let them.

Be yourself and you will attract a man who loves you for you.

Whether you end up in a relationship or not, remember that you are in control of your own life. A relationship is a great add-on to a great life, but it is not the defining factor of your life. The dating process can actually help you learn a lot about yourself so give yourself over to the process and enjoy this time. This time of discovery, this time of meeting new people and having new experiences. It doesn't last forever, and you can create some really beautiful memories from it.

References

Alonzo, C. (2017, June 16). Banishing The Good Girl Complex: The Fears and Growth of a New CEO. Retrieved March 31, 2020, from https://javelina.co/banishing-the-good-girl-complex/

Beck, L. (2017, October 7). 15 Things Women Do That Turn Men Off. Retrieved March 31, 2020, from https://www.cosmopolitan.com/sex-love/news/a48250/real-guys-admit-what-turns-them-off-of-a-girl/

Bolde. (2017, August 1). If You Want Guys To Treat You Better, Start Treating Yourself Better. Retrieved March 31, 2020, from https://www.bolde.com/want-guys-treat-you-better-have-start-treating-yourself/

Brown, L. (2020, March 22). How to tell if a guy likes you: 33 surprising signs he's into you! Retrieved March 31, 2020, from https://hackspirit.com/how-to-tell-if-a-guy-likes-you/

Domelle, A. (2019, January 10). How to set boundaries in relationships without feeling selfish. Retrieved March 31, 2020, from https://medium.com/thrive-global/how-to-set-boundaries-in-relationships-without-feeling-selfish-c95e26d8b3ed

Experts, Y. T. (2018, July 8). 6 Ways Men & Women Communicate Differently. Retrieved March 31, 2020, from https://psychcentral.com/blog/6-ways-men-and-women-communicate-differently/

Fader, S. (2018, May 16). Using Eye Contact Attraction To Build A Relationship. Retrieved March 31, 2020, from https://www.betterhelp.com/advice/attraction/using-eye-contact-attraction-to-build-a-relationship/

Fox, A. S. (2015, March 2). 3 Steps to Making Eye Contact With a Guy Confidently. Retrieved March 31, 2020, from https://verilymag.com/2015/03/the-importance-of-making-eye-contact-dating-relationships

Ghose, M. (2015, January 16). 5 Ways To (Finally) Stop Falling For The Bad Boy. Retrieved March 31, 2020, from https://www.yourtango.com/experts/moushumi-ghose/chasing-bad-boy

Henriques, G. (2016, October 30). Why Communication Between Men and Women Sometimes Fails. Retrieved March 31, 2020, from https://www.psychologytoday.com/us/blog/theory-knowledge/201610/why-communication-between-men-and-women-sometimes-fails

Integration, I. (2018, April 15). 4 Pillars for Recovery After Narcissistic Abuse. Retrieved March 31, 2020, from https://medium.com/@OwnYourReality/4-pillars-for-recovery-after-narcissistic-abuse-7195a40f0b6a

James, S. (2018, May 12). How To Overcome Shyness And Social Anxiety. Retrieved March 31, 2020, from https://projectlifemastery.com/how-to-overcome-shyness-and-social-anxiety/

January 14th, 2013 4 C. (2013, January 14). If you truly love someone, let them be free. Retrieved March 31, 2020, from https://blog.kareldonk.com/if-you-truly-love-someone-let-them-be-free/

Kaplan, J. S., & Tolin, D. F. (2011, September 6). Exposure Therapy for Anxiety Disorders. Retrieved March 31, 2020, from https://www.psychiatrictimes.com/anxiety/exposure-therapy-anxiety-disorders

Lee, L. (2017, December 22). 7 Reasons Why You Shouldn't Lower Your Standards Just Because You Are Single. Retrieved March 31, 2020, from https://herway.net/relationship/7-reasons-shouldnt-lower-standards-just-single/

Lexico. (n.d.). Trust: Definition of Trust by Lexico. Retrieved March 31, 2020, from https://www.lexico.com/en/definition/trust

Lilah. (2018, November 28). 5 Times to Compromise in Your
        Relationship, and 5 Times When You Should Stand Your
        Ground. Retrieved March 31, 2020, from
        https://stylecaster.com/5-times-compromise-in-your-
        relationship-5-times-when-you-should-stand-your-ground/

LoDolce, A. (2019, October 24). How To Choose Between Two Men: 9
        Questions to Ask Yourself. Retrieved March 31, 2020, from
        https://sexyconfidence.com/how-to-choose-between-two-
        men/

LoDolce, A. (2019, October 24). What to Talk About With a Guy: 18
        Things That Keep Him Interested. Retrieved March 31, 2020,
        from https://sexyconfidence.com/what-to-talk-about-with-a-
        guy/

LoDolce, A. (2019, October 24). 15 Signs He's Using You and What You
        Can Do About it. Retrieved March 31, 2020, from
        https://sexyconfidence.com/signs-hes-using-you/

LoDolce, A. (2019, October 24). How To Tell If a Guy Likes You: 11
        Proven Signs He Is Into You! Retrieved March 31, 2020, from
        https://sexyconfidence.com/how-to-tell-if-a-guy-likes-you/

LovePanky. (2015, May 3). How to Talk to a Guy and Make Him Like You.
        Retrieved March 31, 2020, from
        https://www.lovepanky.com/women/attracting-and-dating-
        men/how-to-talk-to-a-guy-you-like

Mary, S. (2018, March 14). Letting Go of the "Good Girl" Complex.
        Retrieved March 31, 2020, from
        https://medium.com/@sarahmaryzimmerman/letting-go-of-
        the-good-girl-complex-55a633c03cb0

Morningstar, A. (2020, January 6). 12 Boundaries You Ought To Set In
        Your Relationship. Retrieved March 31, 2020, from
        https://www.aconsciousrethink.com/6573/boundaries-in-
        relationships/

Naik, S., Martinez, P., & Hampton, T. (2018, July 31). 15 Signs A Guy Is
        Using You For Sex, Money, Ego, Favors etc. Retrieved March
        31, 2020, from https://www.luvze.com/signs-a-guy-is-using-

you/

Newsonen, S. (2018, February 21). 5 Ways to Escape 'Good-Girl Syndrome'. Retrieved March 31, 2020, from https://www.psychologytoday.com/us/blog/the-path-passionate-happiness/201802/5-ways-escape-good-girl-syndrome

Phillips, R. R. (2019, May 28). How to Choose Between your Boyfriend and Another Guy: Part 1 & 2. Retrieved March 31, 2020, from http://talkaboutluv.com/how-to-choose-between-your-boyfriend-and-another-guy/

Posted December 12, 2017 by admin/ P. R. and A. (2019, May 2). Gender Differences in Communication Styles: PPU online. Retrieved March 31, 2020, from https://online.pointpark.edu/public-relations-and-advertising/gender-differences-communication-styles/

Psychology Today. (2018, July 2). Don't Tell Me What to Do! Retrieved March 31, 2020, from https://www.psychologytoday.com/intl/blog/love-cycles-fear-cycles/201807/don-t-tell-me-what-do

Rova, A. (2019, July 29). 4 Practical Steps to Setting Boundaries with Men. Retrieved March 31, 2020, from https://medium.com/@annarova/4-practical-steps-to-setting-boundaries-with-men-bae82f20d3aa

Rova, A. (2019, October 19). Set Your Man Free: A Practical Guide to a Thriving Relationship with Him & Yourself. Retrieved March 31, 2020, from https://medium.com/girlskill/set-your-man-free-a-practical-guide-to-a-thriving-relationship-with-him-yourself-a9b8b3315246

Sama, J. M. (2019, November 6). The Top 12 Qualities Men Want in a Woman. Retrieved March 31, 2020, from https://goodmenproject.com/featured-content/the-top-12-qualities-men-want-in-a-woman-dg/

Star, C. (2018, July 8). Boundaries: Learn How to Stand Your Ground. Retrieved March 31, 2020, from https://psychcentral.com/blog/boundaries-learn-how-to-stand-your-ground/

Stillman, J. (2012, July 9). Too Shy? 3 Tricks to Beat Social Anxiety. Retrieved March 31, 2020, from https://www.inc.com/jessica-stillman/tricks-for-overcoming-social-anxiety-shyness.html

Tapley, B. (2018, January 23). 10 Things That Turn Men Off. Retrieved March 31, 2020, from https://www.womansday.com/relationships/dating-marriage/advice/a1388/10-things-that-turn-men-off-104649/

Tartakovsky, M. (2018, July 8). What It Means to Teach People How to Treat You. Retrieved March 31, 2020, from https://psychcentral.com/blog/what-it-means-to-teach-people-how-to-treat-you/

This Way Up. (n.d.). I Feel Shy. Retrieved March 31, 2020, from https://thiswayup.org.au/how-do-you-feel/shy/

Thought Catalog. (2016, December 21). 10 Reasons Why You Should Never (Ever!) Settle In Love. Retrieved March 31, 2020, from https://thoughtcatalog.com/amy-spencer/2016/12/10-reasons-why-you-should-never-ever-settle-in-love/

Tuccinard, R. (n.d.). 7 Ways to Stop Falling for the Same Type of Guy. Retrieved March 31, 2020, from https://www.hercampus.com/sex-relationships/relationships/7-ways-stop-falling-same-type-guy

Wygant, D. (2014, September 7). Why You Must Surrender and Let Him Go. Retrieved March 31, 2020, from https://www.huffpost.com/entry/why-you-must-surrender-an_b_5561870

Xepoleas, S. (n.d.). Sex in society: Stigmas and realities. Retrieved March 31, 2020, from https://theorion.com/46128/features/sex-in-society-stigmas-and-realities/

Your Courageous Life. (n.d.). making your own rules. Retrieved March 31, 2020, from https://www.yourcourageouslife.com/category/making-your-own-rules/

www.ingramcontent.com/pod-product-compliance
Lightning Source LLC
Chambersburg PA
CBHW051458250726
48655CB00001B/474